the drawings of Rodin

Introduction by

STEPHEN LONGSTREET

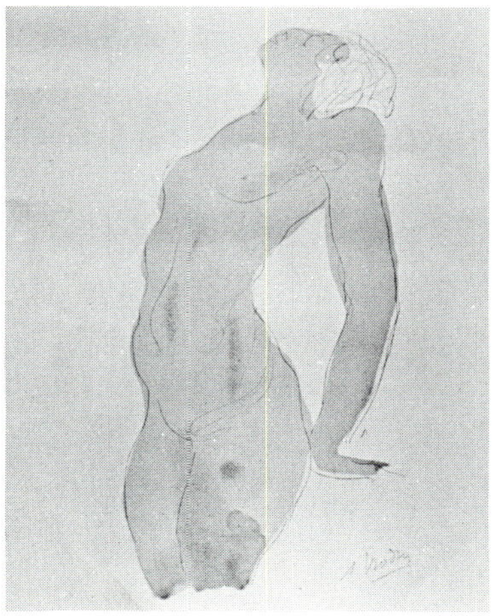

BORDEN PUBLISHING COMPANY
ALHAMBRA, CALIFORNIA

FIRST EDITION

PRINTED IN THE UNITED STATES OF AMERICA

FRANCOIS AUGUSTE RENE RODIN

1840-1917

All the best works of any artist must be bathed in mystery.
RODIN

AT THE AGE OF NINE, a short stocky child of the Paris streets, he was already drawing, given to pleasure at the sight of the human body, not interested in buildings, landscapes, or dead eatable game or softening fruit that others used as subjects for art. He was a poor student; some blamed this on his myopia, but nothing stopped him drawing. He attended the 'Petite Ecole', loved the Louvre and the engravings of Italian masters at the Bibliothèque Imperiale. At fifteen he won a bronze medal for his drawings from casts and entered the studio of a sculptor called Fort. At seventeen he won first and second class medals for modeling and drawing. He delighted in working from the nude model.

His early work impressed men and artists important in their day and they advised him to try and get into the Ecole des Beaux Arts. He made three unsuccessful attempts. This failure was depressing for without the official school background the hope of a young artist to exhibit in the salons was zero. Oddly enough this soon-to-be-great sculptor passed his drawing tests *but* failed in modeling. He became a handyman, mixing plaster, pulling casts for decor. His struggle was long and hard.

It was not till 1877, when he showed his statue of a nude man called *The Age of Bronze,* that fame came to him. But with fame came attacks claiming no man could model so life-like a statue; he *must* have made plaster casts of a real human being.

Slowly, then faster, he became the great master, the maker of hundreds of over-life-sized figures; those exotic embracing lovers, hands of God, the magnificent Balzacs, and the giant labor which was never fulfilled—the great plaster model of Dante's *Gates of Hell,* from which *The Thinker* comes.

What is important to us is that he never stopped making drawings. At no time in his life did Rodin remain only the sculptor. His pencil was never far away, and on paper he dreamed, improbable monuments, exalted riders on great steeds, the interplay of heroic bodies, *and* those fascinating drawings of dancing figures that have been so copied and forged. He called his drawings "from nature" and nature was the body naked or slightly draped. He made a few architectural sketches for his *Gates,* but the rest of his draftsmanship he used on the body.

His drawings of the 1870s and 80s are monumental; battling figures, gods, riders, murderers. Done in ink and gouache they are often almost solid silhouettes. These are works of fantasy and not like his later work when the mind and eye and hand moved closer to the figures in the scene at play or posing. "My models wander naked in the studio." Gone are the sources of Canto XVI of Dante's *Inferno.* He was becoming interested in the play of limbs without literary content. Yet we must not overlook the great early period; it is seldom known to the art student who is often aware only of the later drawings in a different vein. What is interesting is that Rodin hardly ever uses his drawings to make sculpture, but he often draws from his finished models or carvings. His drawing is not a testing of sculpture but an art in its own right.

He was not for using his models in stiff studio poses but kept them moving freely about the place, or in gardens and woods, trying to catch the grace of easy patterns made by people, not attempting to reproduce something seen in ballet or in old Greek marbles. He drew without looking at the paper, keeping his eyes on the model. "The moment I drop my eye, the flow stops . . . my drawings are only a way of testing myself . . . my object is to test to what extent my hand already feels what my eyes see."

In the 1880s he drew contour designs for Baudelaire's poems: *Flowers of Evil,* changing his style to a flat statement, leaving out modeled illusions of deepness, of space. He became very Japanese in his ability to place a figure on paper leaving out background and surrounding space. By the 90s he was flowing a thin wash of some simple color over his pencil or ink line, giving it the magic of volume, of moving and living matter. When carried away, he would make drawing after drawing, dropping them one by one on the floor, never looking at the paper, his eyes glued on the models, moving around, dancing, talking, locking their limbs in play, teasing each other, while the master, his great beard in disorder, shouted to them to pay him no mind, just to go about their business of being.

He drew inspiration from Isadora Duncan, Loie Fuller, Cambodian ritual dancers and he had the touring Royal Troup perform in his house hour after hour while he sketched them.

His late drawings are marvelous examples of suggestion, of draftsmanship, breaking free of the controls and the rules of art schools and teachers. The pencil follows his eye, the suggestion is all, the line lashes like a whip, caresses like a flower. The final transparent wash brings it all to life as living flesh; what we have is the vision of a great master who found in man and woman everything in art. He needed no flowing rivers, fruits or flowers, no green fields, no skies, noble trees.

His power to foreshorten a figure in a drawing is astounding, his ability with nothing but a pencil to capture movement, one version of reality, the human being in his skin acting out his place on earth, his relationship to other bodies. Rodin worked small, usually ten inches by twelve inches (suspect anything larger as perhaps a forgery). His work does not date, for he put no grand technique, no tricky style into his drawings. The simplest forms please him. Nothing extra is needed. He is not trying to appear fancy, or shock as a mannerist. The taste is perfect, something that cannot be said of some of his sculpture. The content of a drawing is rich without being cloying. Literature, which spoils some of his statues, is not here. There is no philosophy to become banal, no ideas taken from books to go out of fashion.

Matisse and Munch were to borrow a great deal from Rodin's drawings—the line wandering almost out of control, the enclosing of an emotion with the pencil's probings, the making of a statement directly, without scratching, rubbing or refining. Much came from Rodin's drawings into modern art. Yet he was a product of his times, and so he defended the idea that the drawings were not just drawings: "It is a false idea that drawing itself can be beautiful. It is only beautiful through the truths and the feelings it translates."

His range is wide, even copies after Michelangelo and the Medici tombs. These are now in the Musée Rodin where there are about seven thousand of his drawings. At least two hundred are always on exhibit, on view to the public. He is buried here on the grounds of the museum, once the Hotel Biron. *The Thinker* serves as a marker of his grave. He died of pneumonia during the dark years of a dismal war, on a cold November day in 1917. In a heatless Paris, his great work done. His bier held honors: a doctoral robe from Oxford, the Knights Cross of the Legion of Honor. What he said of Michelangelo can be said of him. "Art did not content him. He wanted infinity."

STEPHEN LONGSTREET

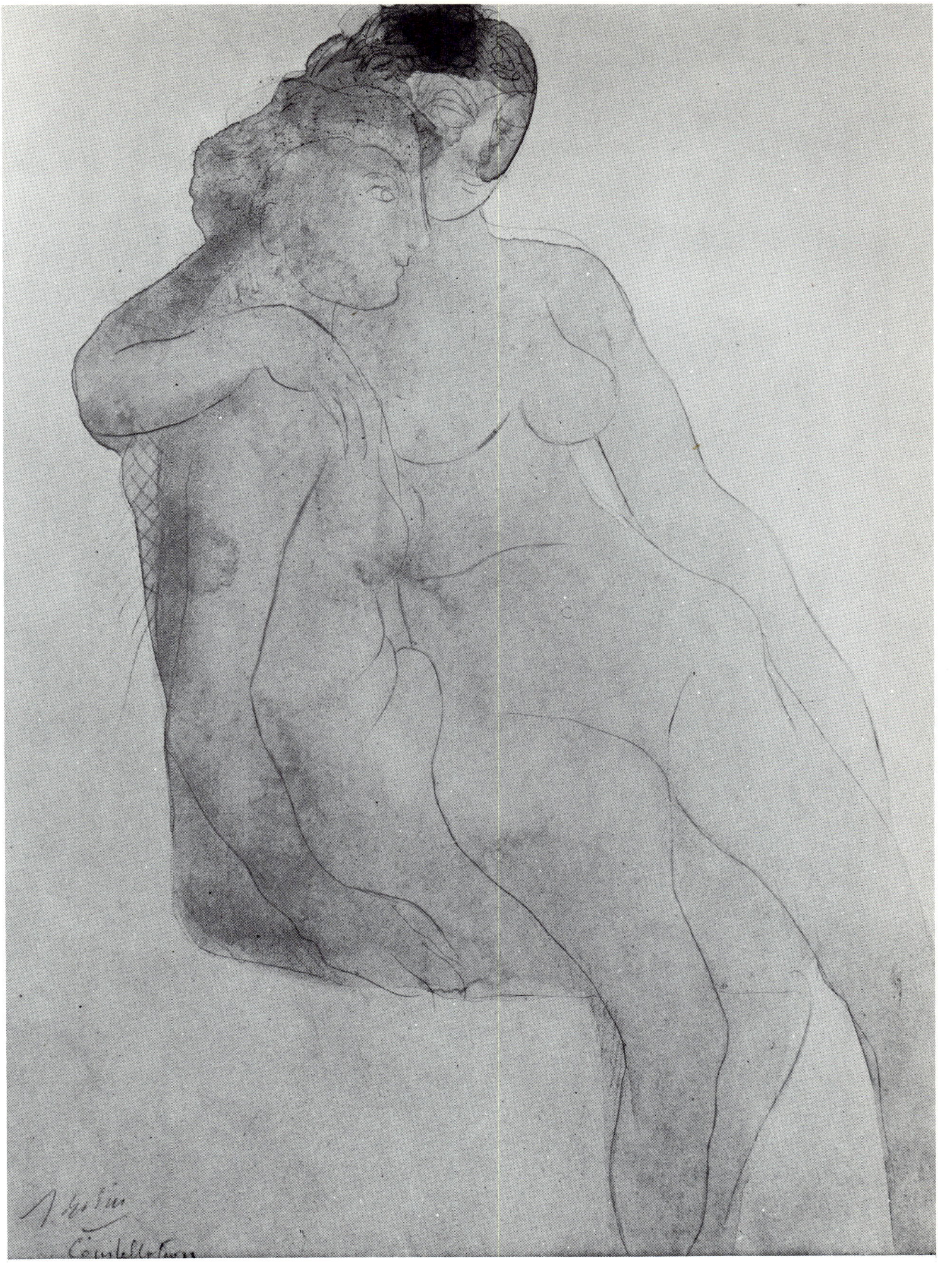

Constellation

Pencil and wash

THE BOURDELLE MUSEUM, PARIS, FRANCE

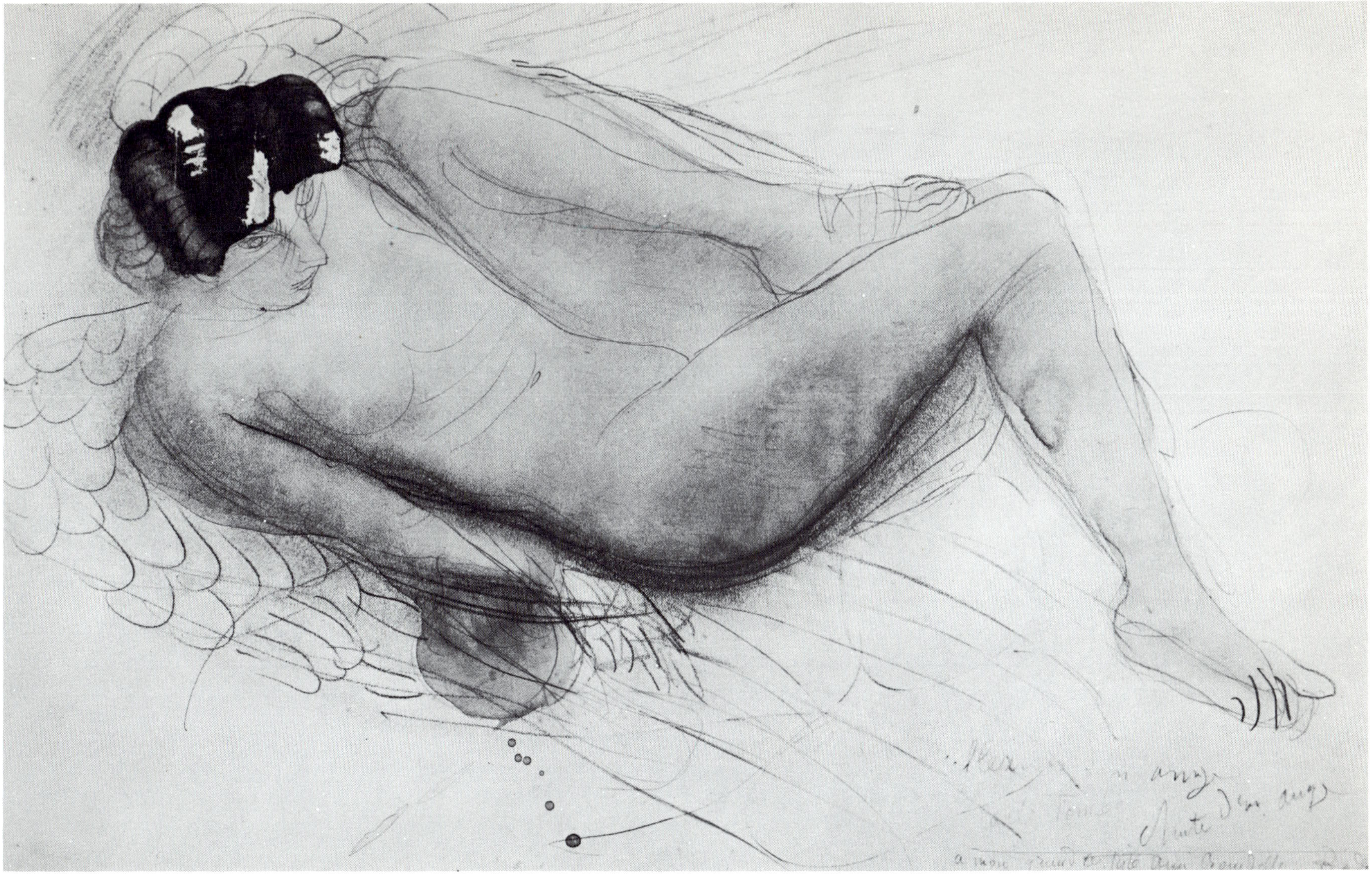

A Fallen Angel

Pencil and watercolor

THE BOURDELLE MUSEUM, PARIS, FRANCE

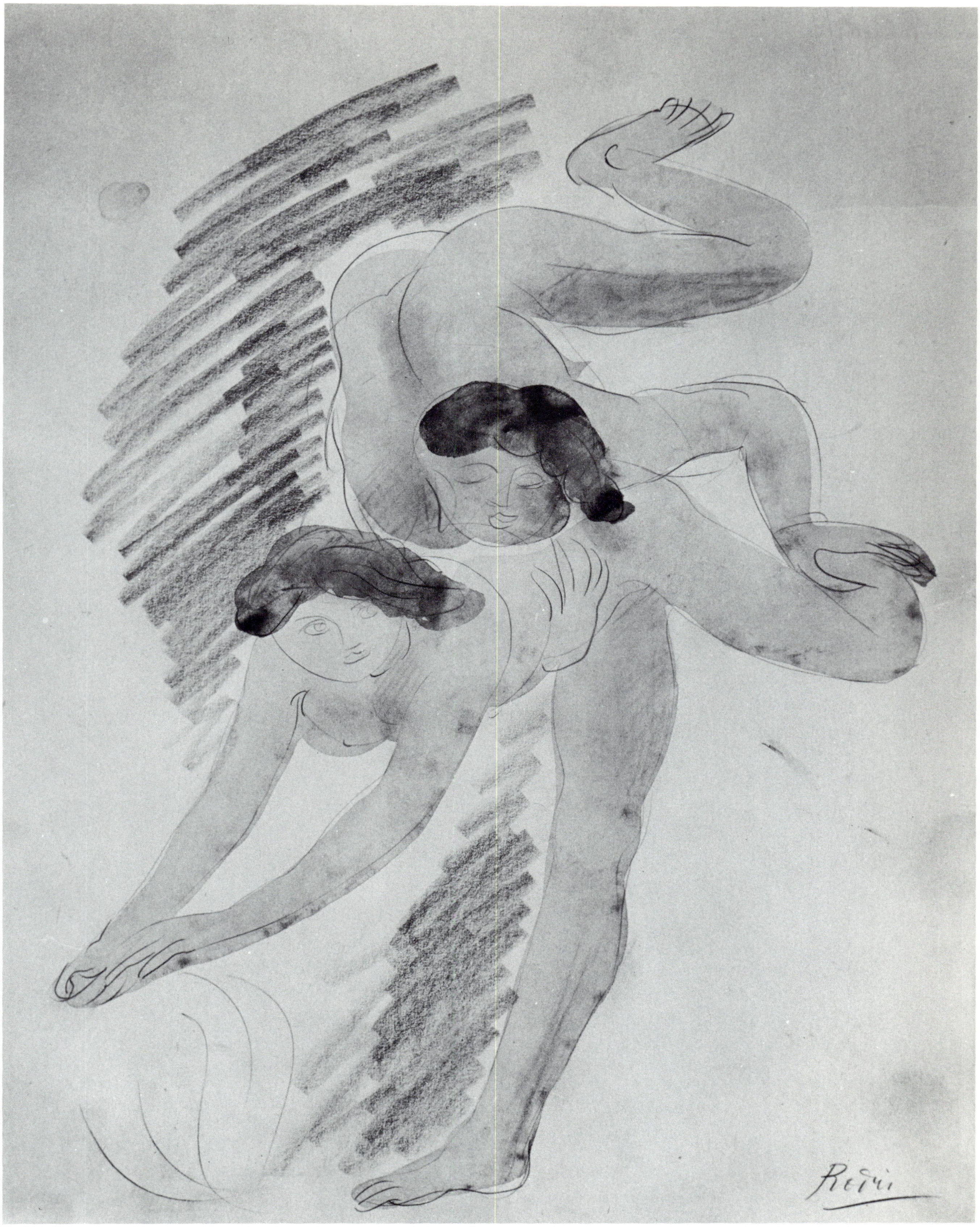

Two Figure Studies

Pencil, pen and ink, crayon and pink wash

COURTESY MARY PICKFORD, BEVERLY HILLS, CALIFORNIA

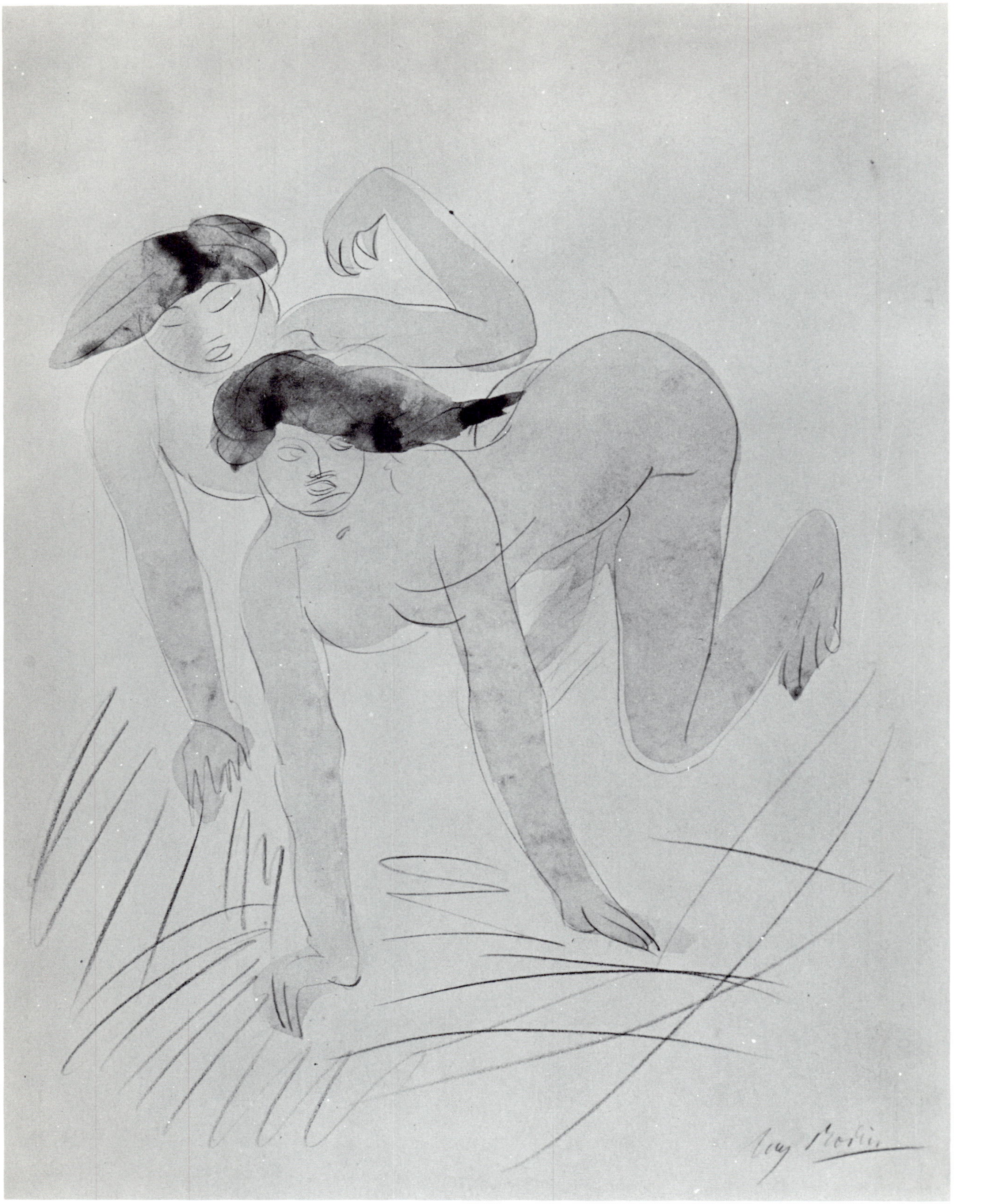

Two Kneeling Figures

Pencil, pen and ink, crayon and pink wash

COURTESY MARY PICKFORD, BEVERLY HILLS, CALIFORNIA

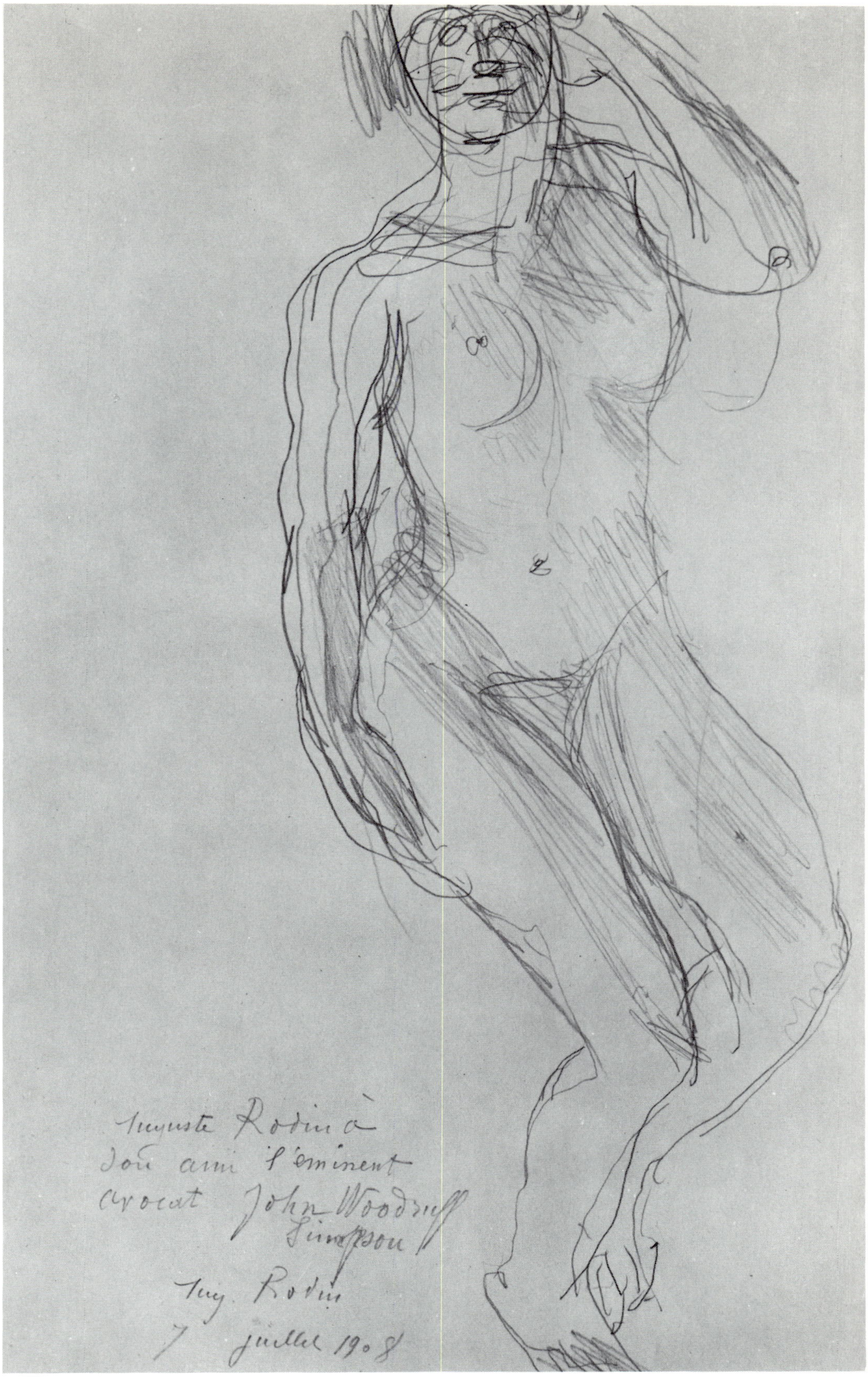

Seated Female Nude

Pencil

NATIONAL GALLERY OF ART, WASHINGTON, D.C.

ROSENWALD COLLECTION

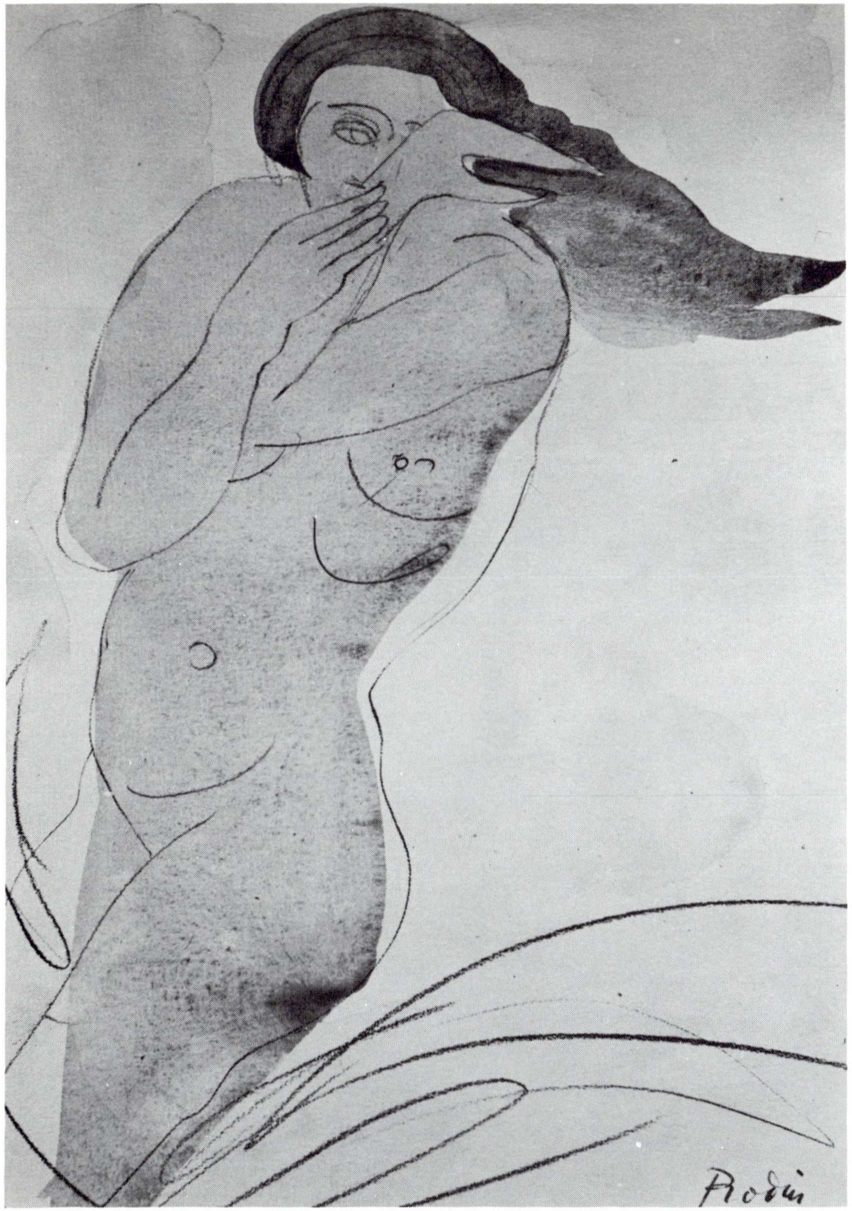

Female Nude

Pencil, pink and gray watercolor

SANTA BARBARA MUSEUM OF ART, SANTA BARBARA, CALIFORNIA

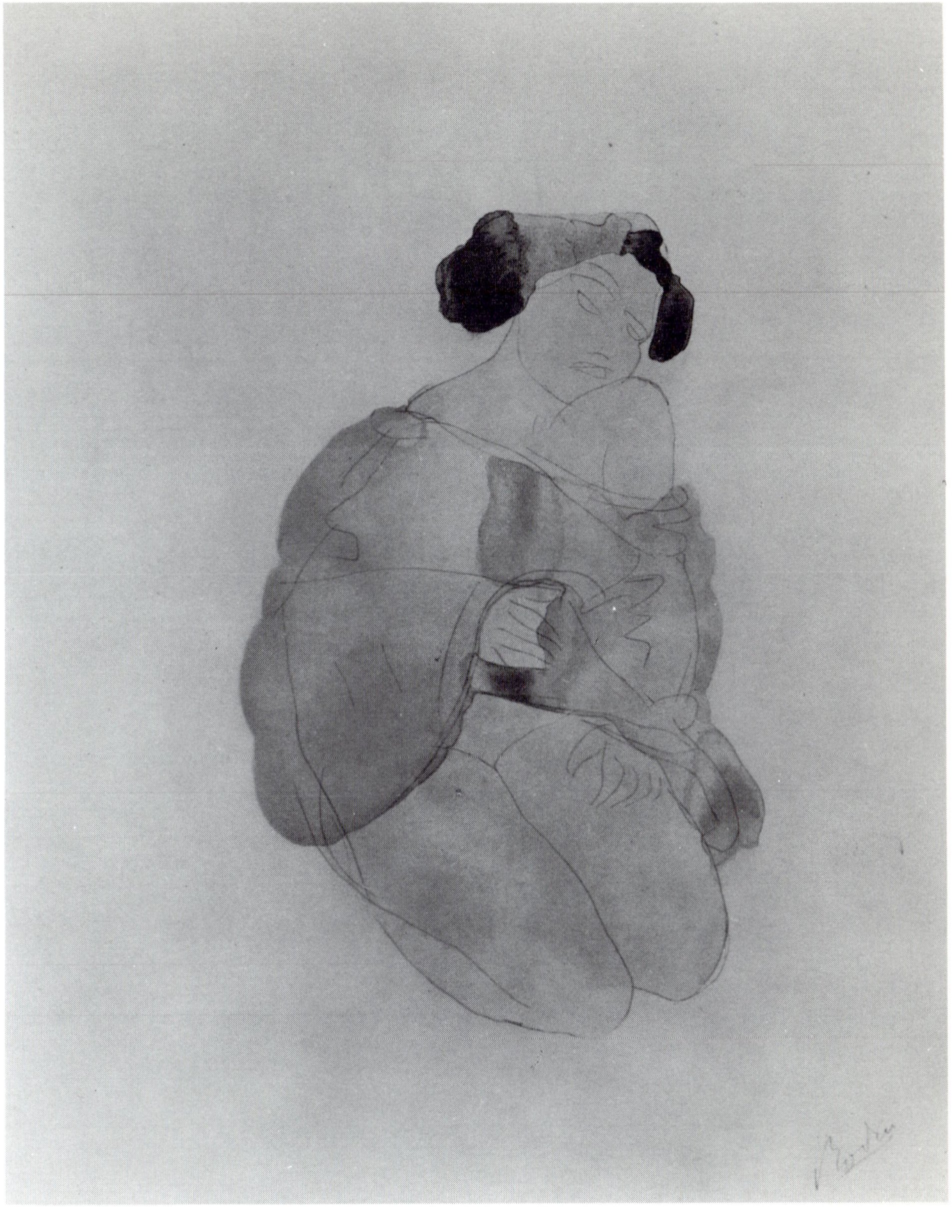

Kneeling Figure

Pencil and wash

CHARLES E. SLATKIN GALLERIES, NEW YORK CITY, N.Y.

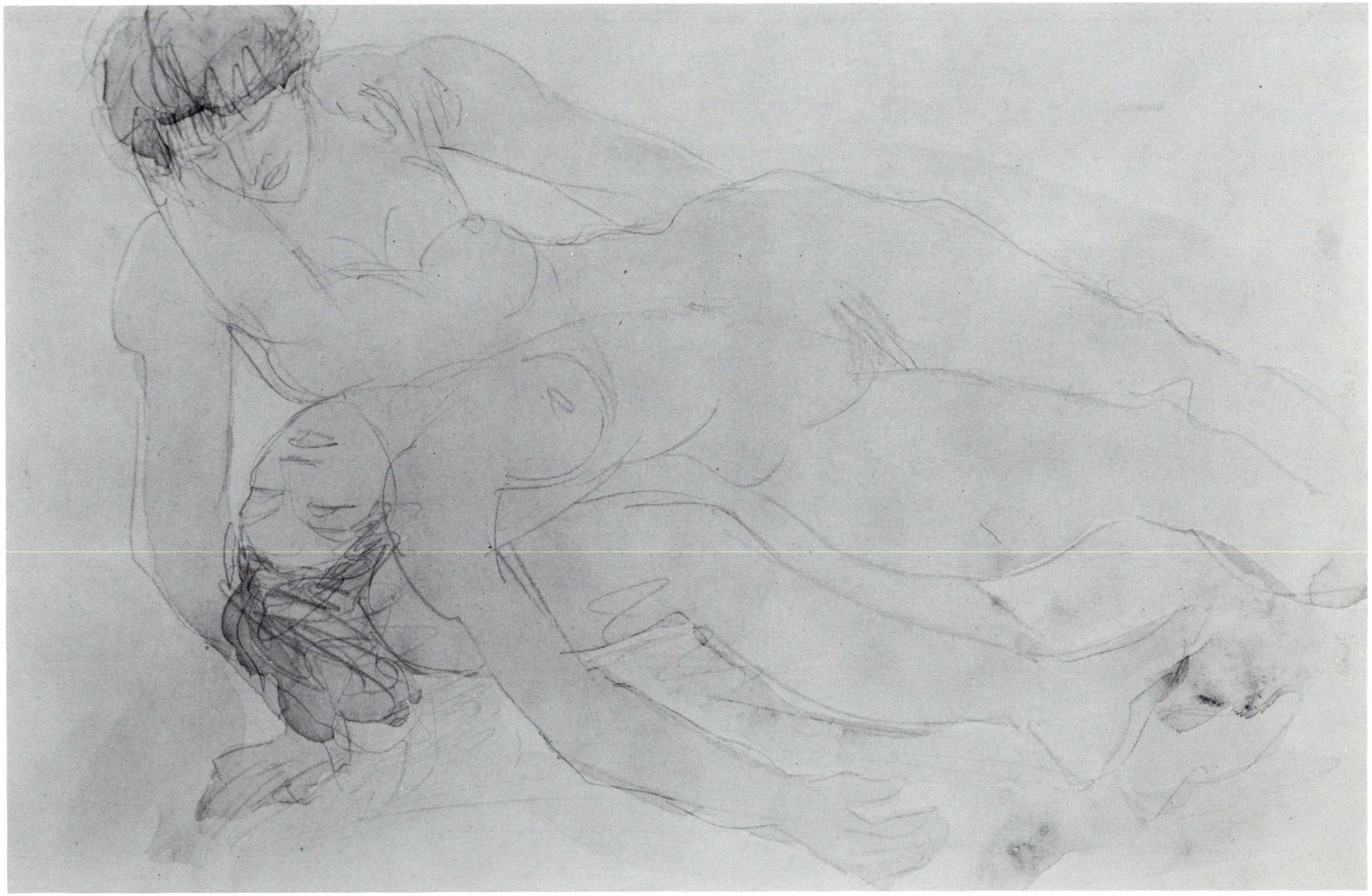

Two Nudes

Pencil and wash

CHARLES E. SLATKIN GALLERIES, NEW YORK CITY, N.Y.

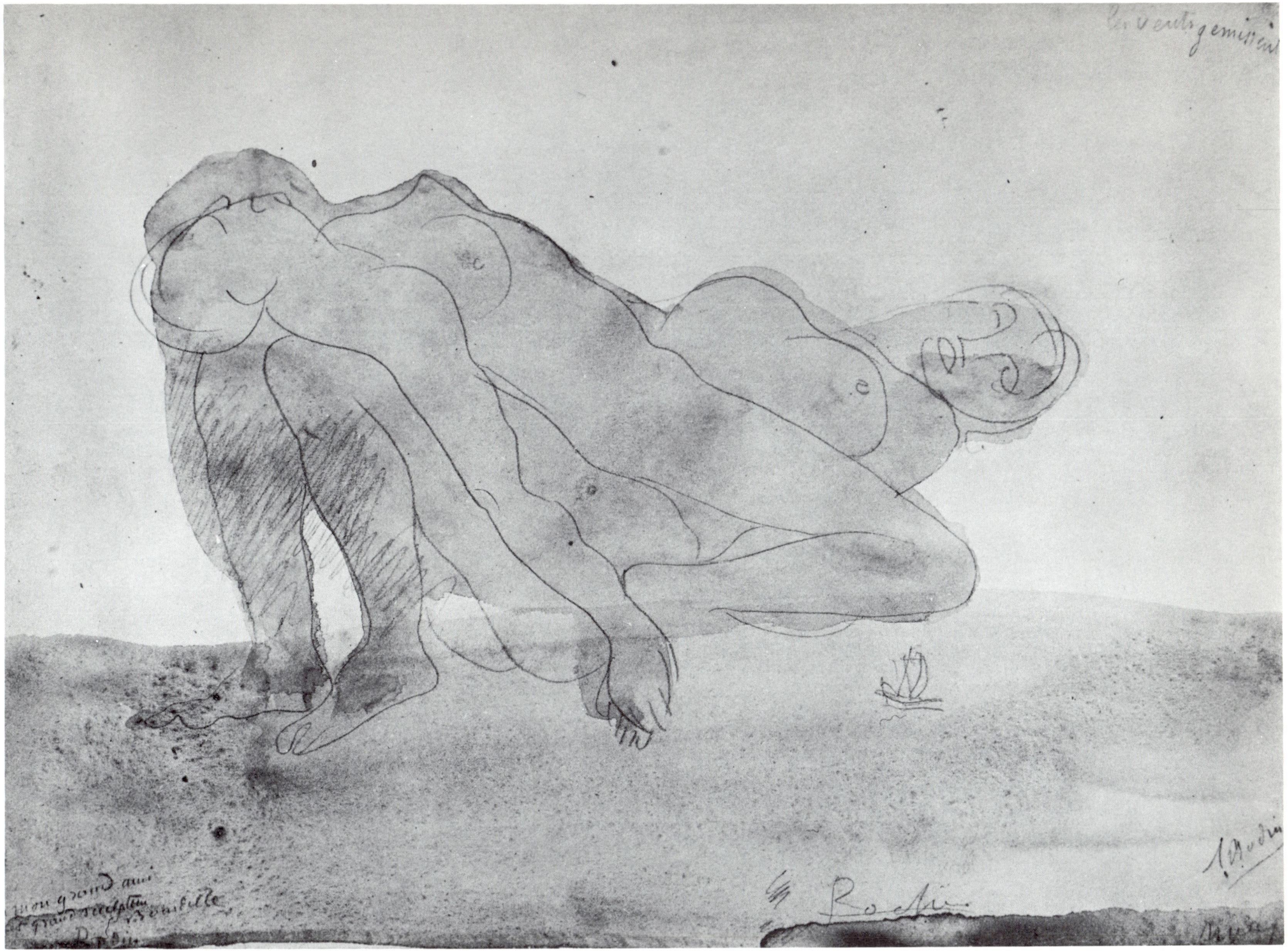

The Winds Wail

Pencil and watercolor

THE BOURDELLE MUSEUM, PARIS, FRANCE

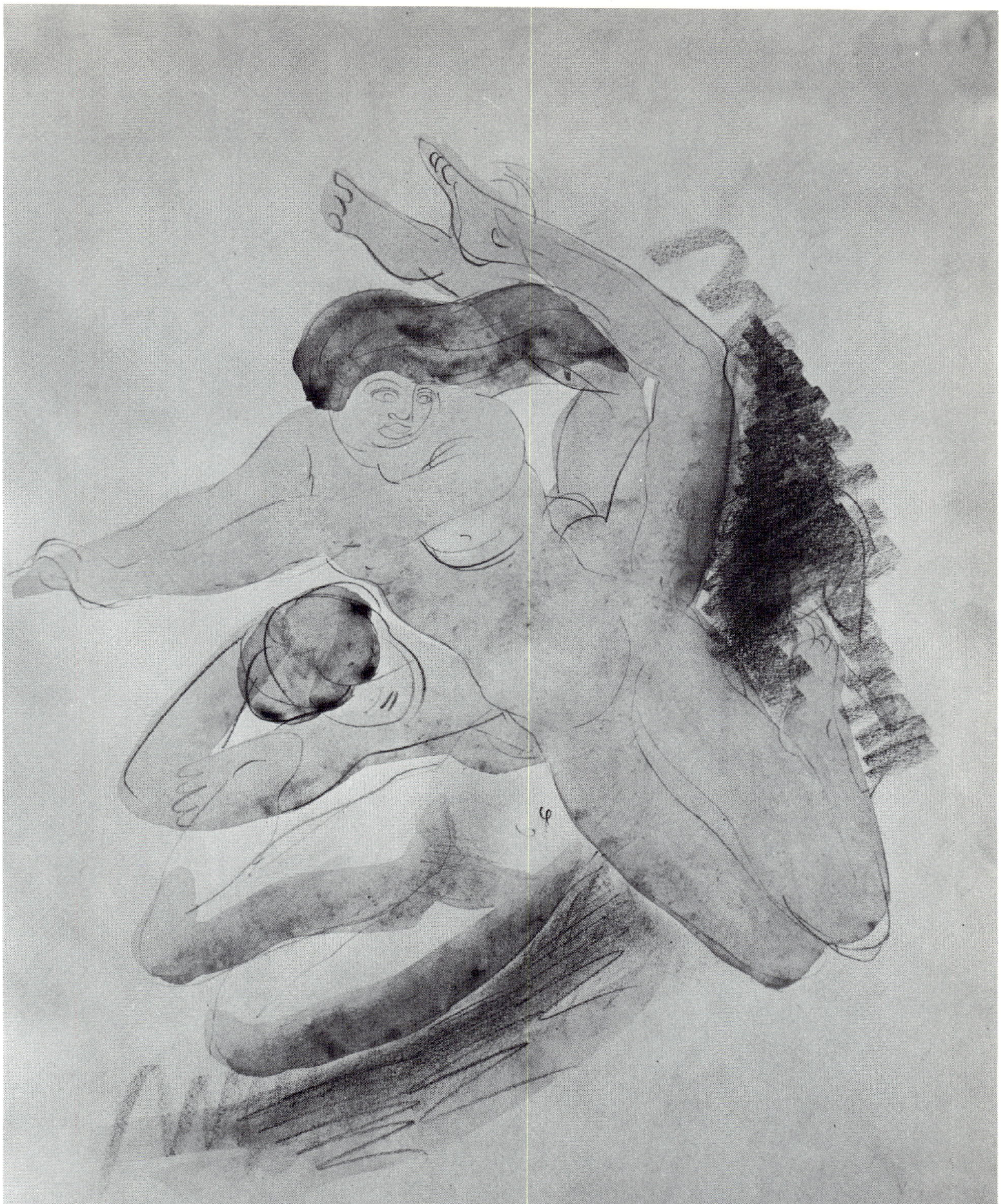

Three Figures in Motion

Pencil, pen and ink, crayon and pink wash

COURTESY MARY PICKFORD, BEVERLY HILLS, CALIFORNIA

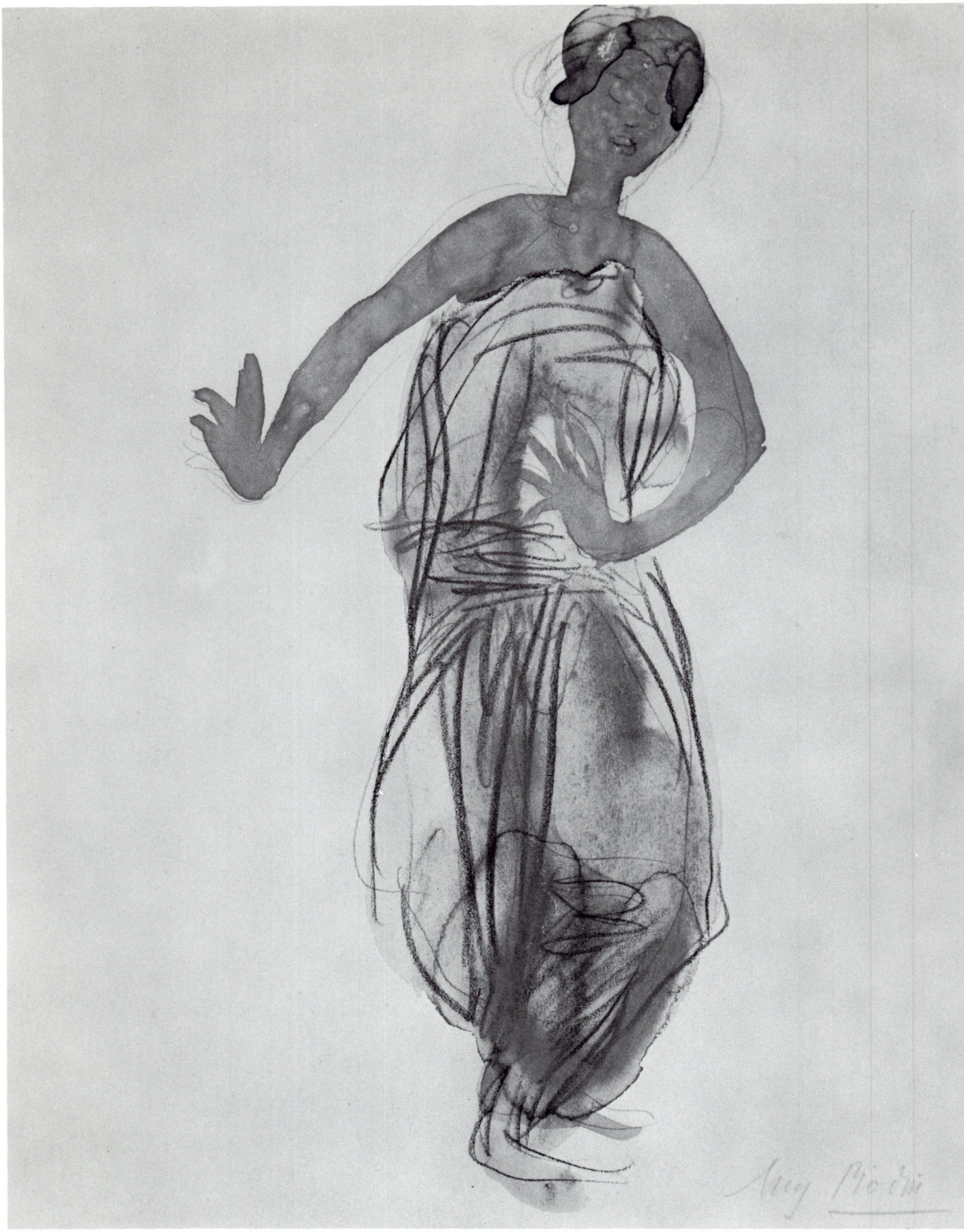

Cambodian Dancer

Watercolor, crayon and pencil

MUSEUM OF FINE ARTS, BOSTON, MASS.

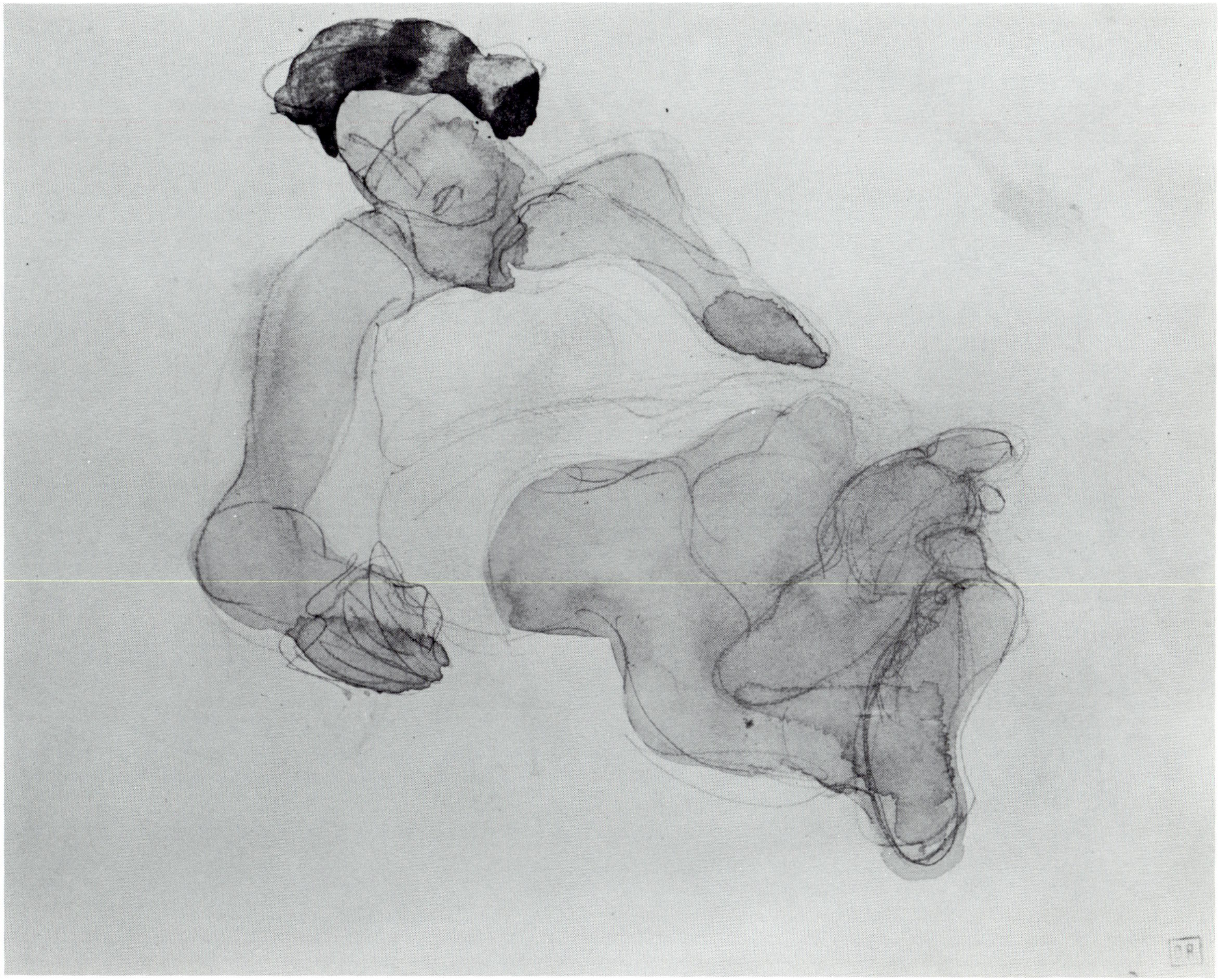

Reclining Nude

Watercolor over pencil

CHARLES E. SLATKIN GALLERIES, NEW YORK CITY, N.Y.

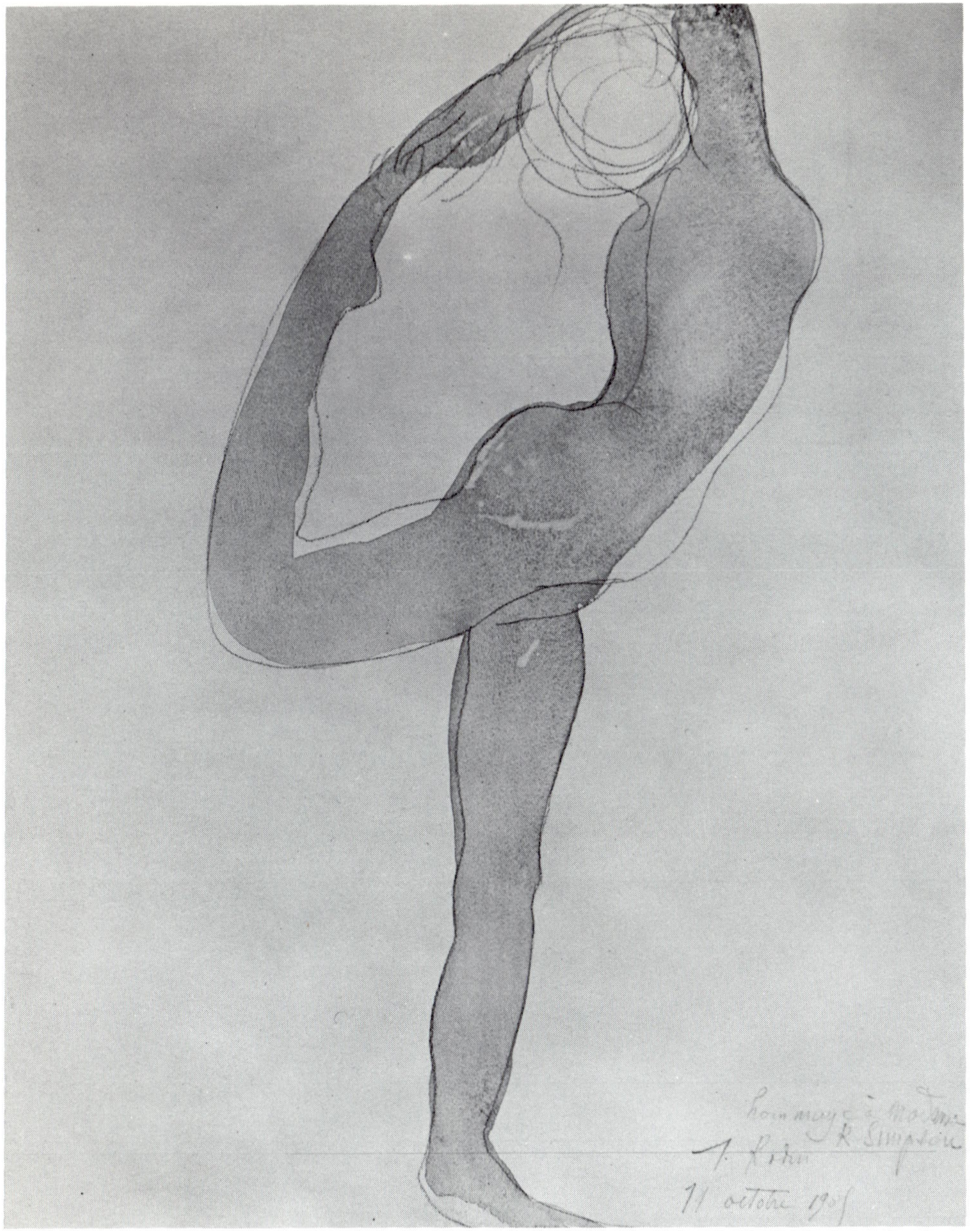

Dancing Figure

Pencil and colored wash

NATIONAL GALLERY OF ART, WASHINGTON, D.C.
SIMPSON COLLECTION

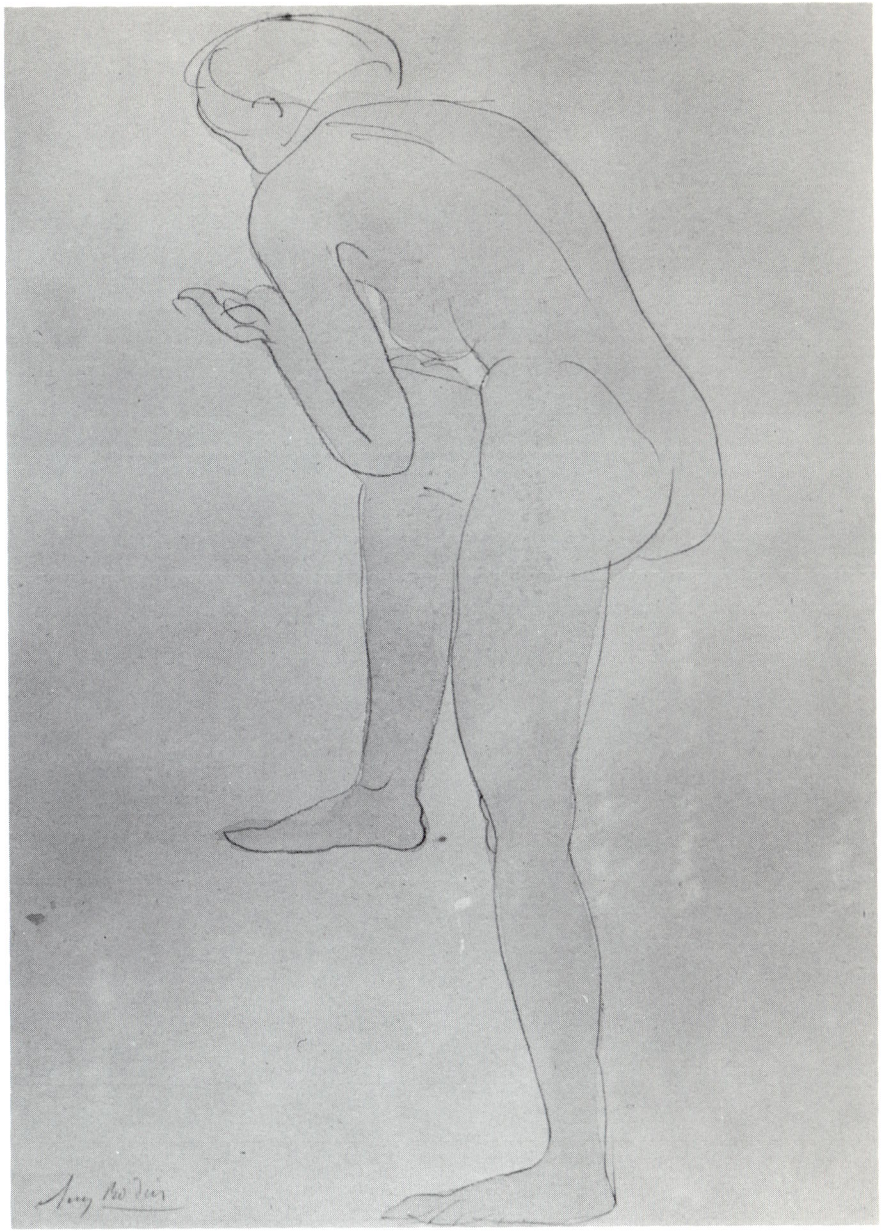

Figure Bending Forward

Pencil and wash

NATIONAL GALLERY OF ART, WASHINGTON, D.C.
SIMPSON COLLECTION

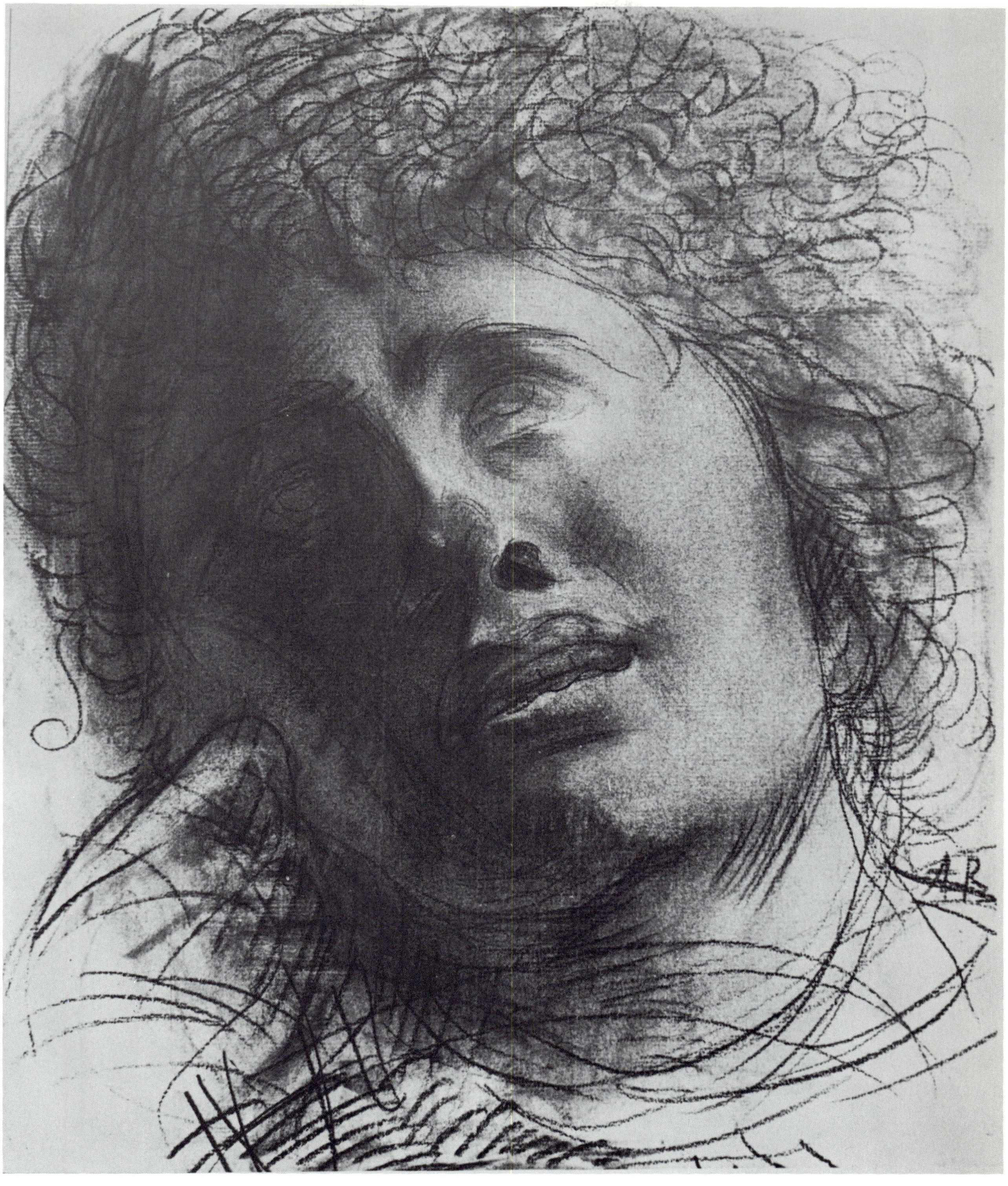

Head Study

Black crayon

MUSEUM OF FINE ARTS, BUDAPEST, HUNGARY

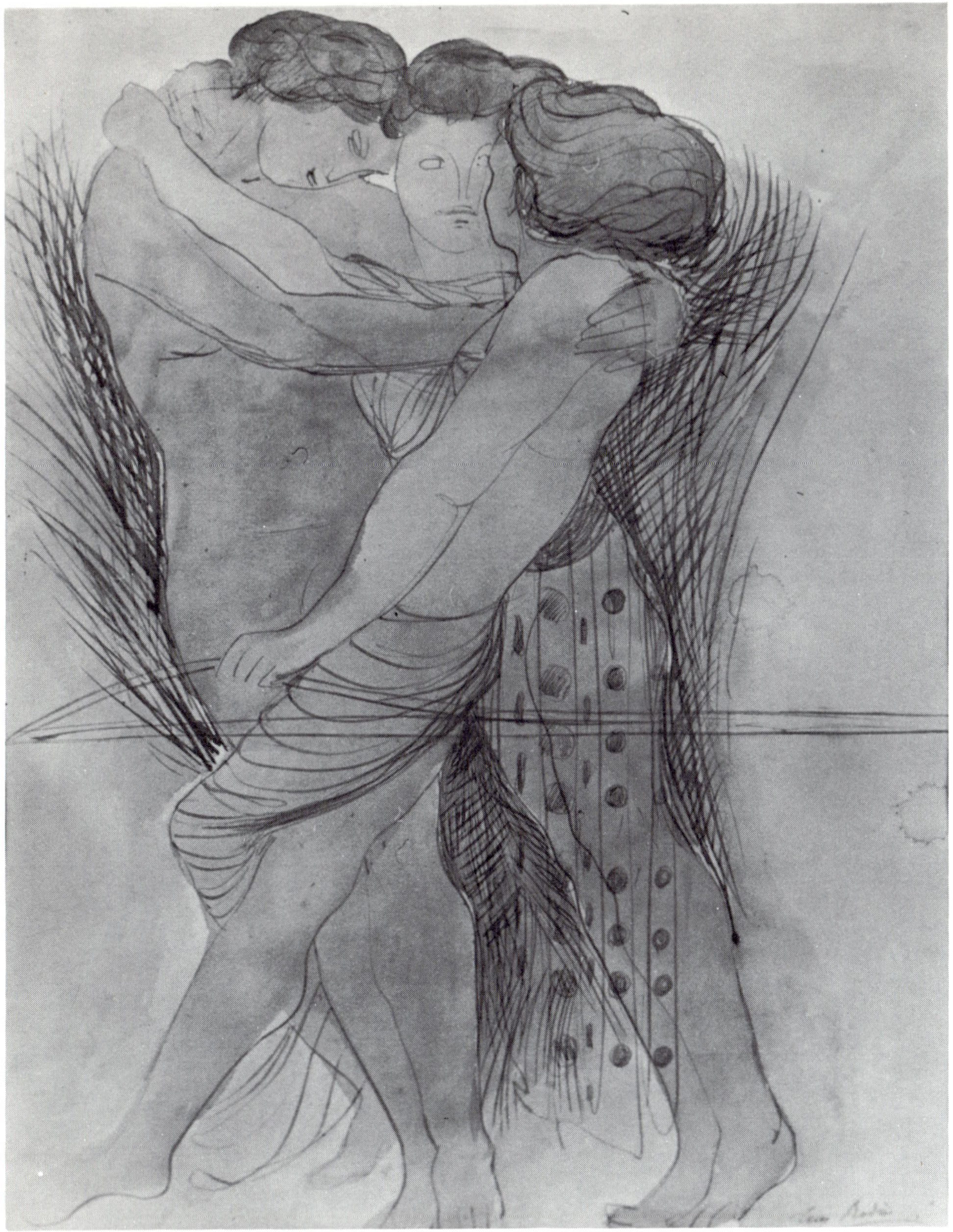

Three Graces

Pen and ink watercolor

COLLECTION OF T. E. HANLEY, BRADFORD, PA.

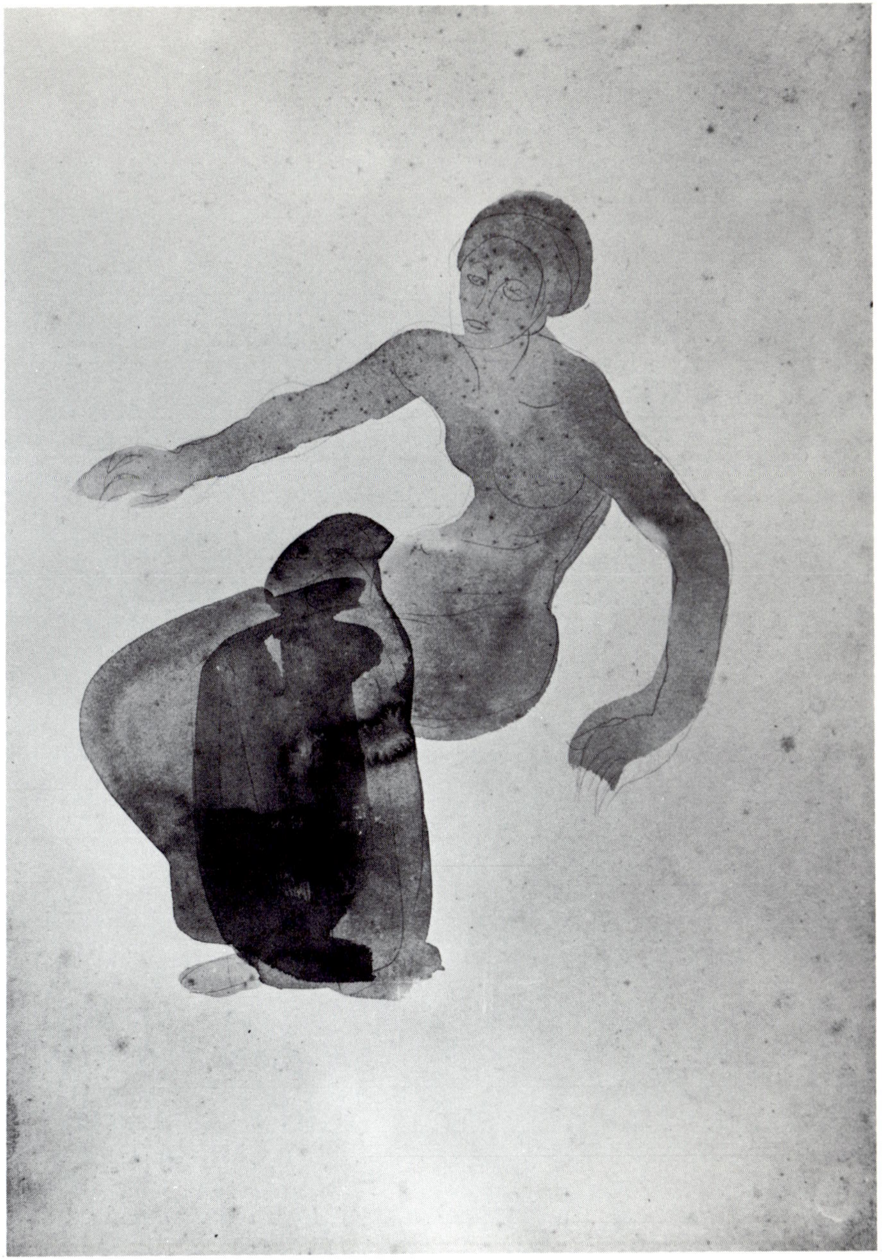

Turbaned Woman

Pencil and watercolor

BOURDELLE MUSEUM, PARIS, FRANCE

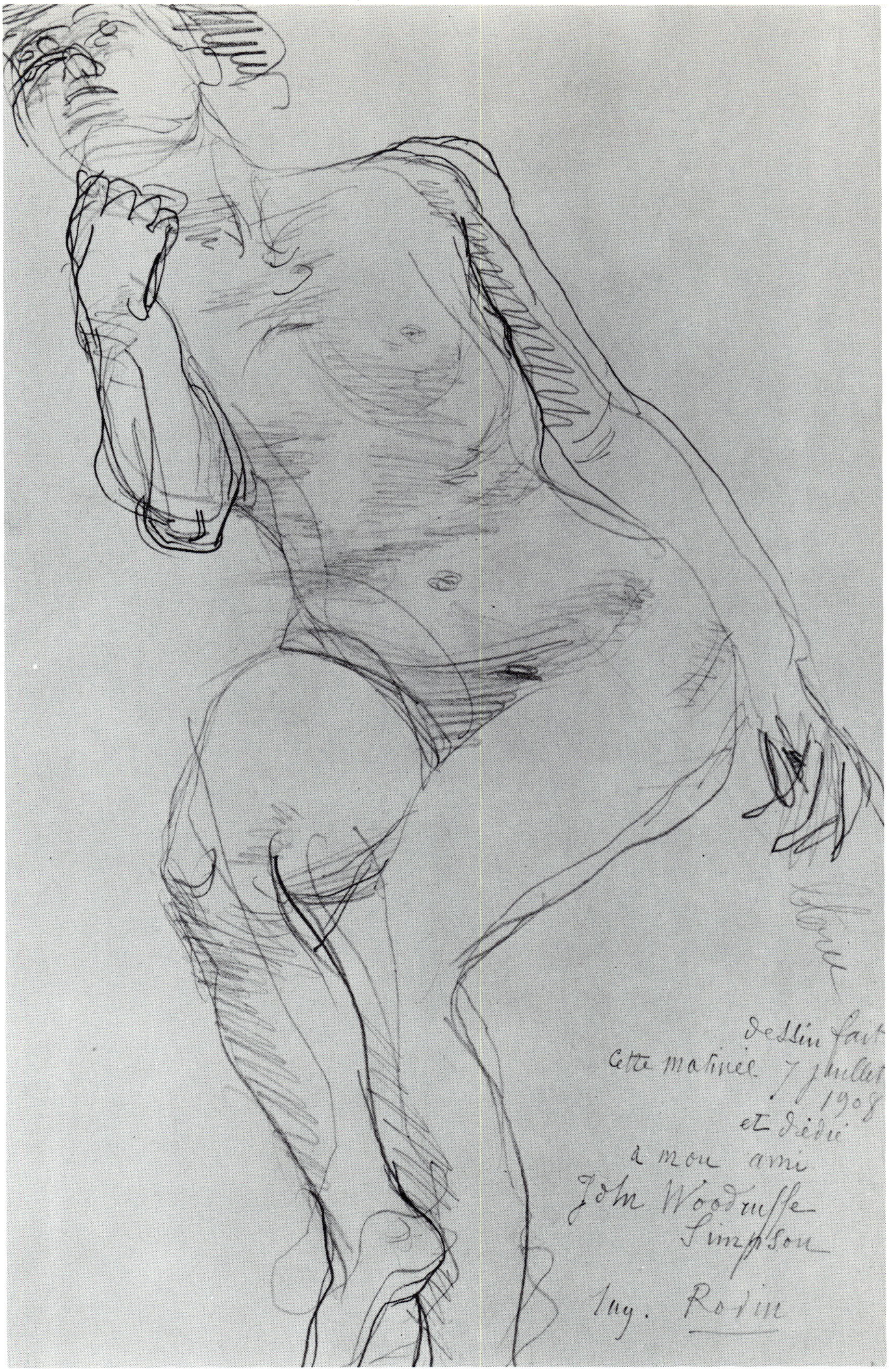

Seated Woman

Pencil

NATIONAL GALLERY OF ART, WASHINGTON, D.C.
ROSENWALD COLLECTION

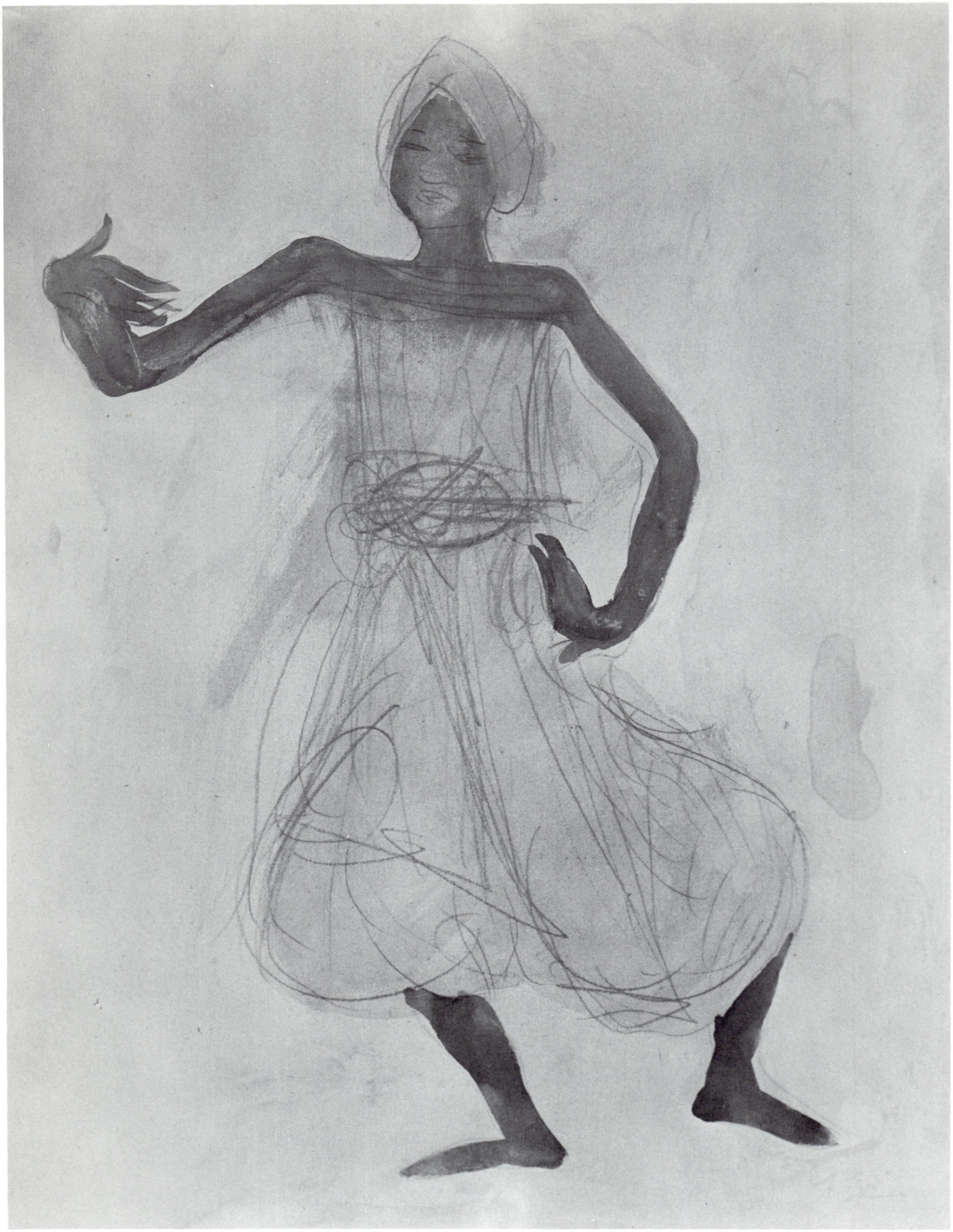

Dancer Facing Front

Pencil and watercolor

CHARLES E. SLATKIN GALLERIES, NEW YORK CITY, N.Y.

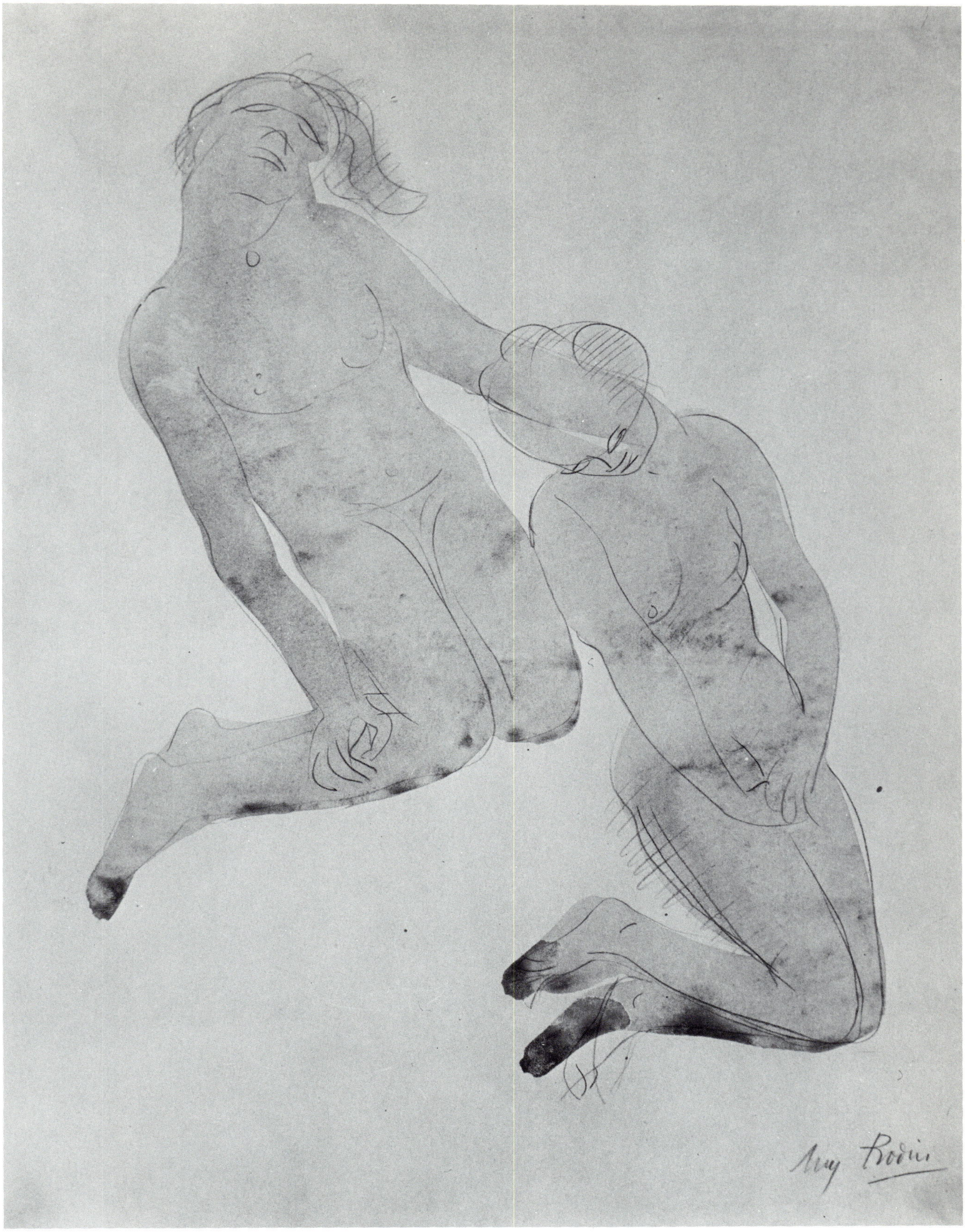

Two Kneeling Nudes

Pencil and pink wash

COURTESY MARY PICKFORD, BEVERLY HILLS, CALIFORNIA

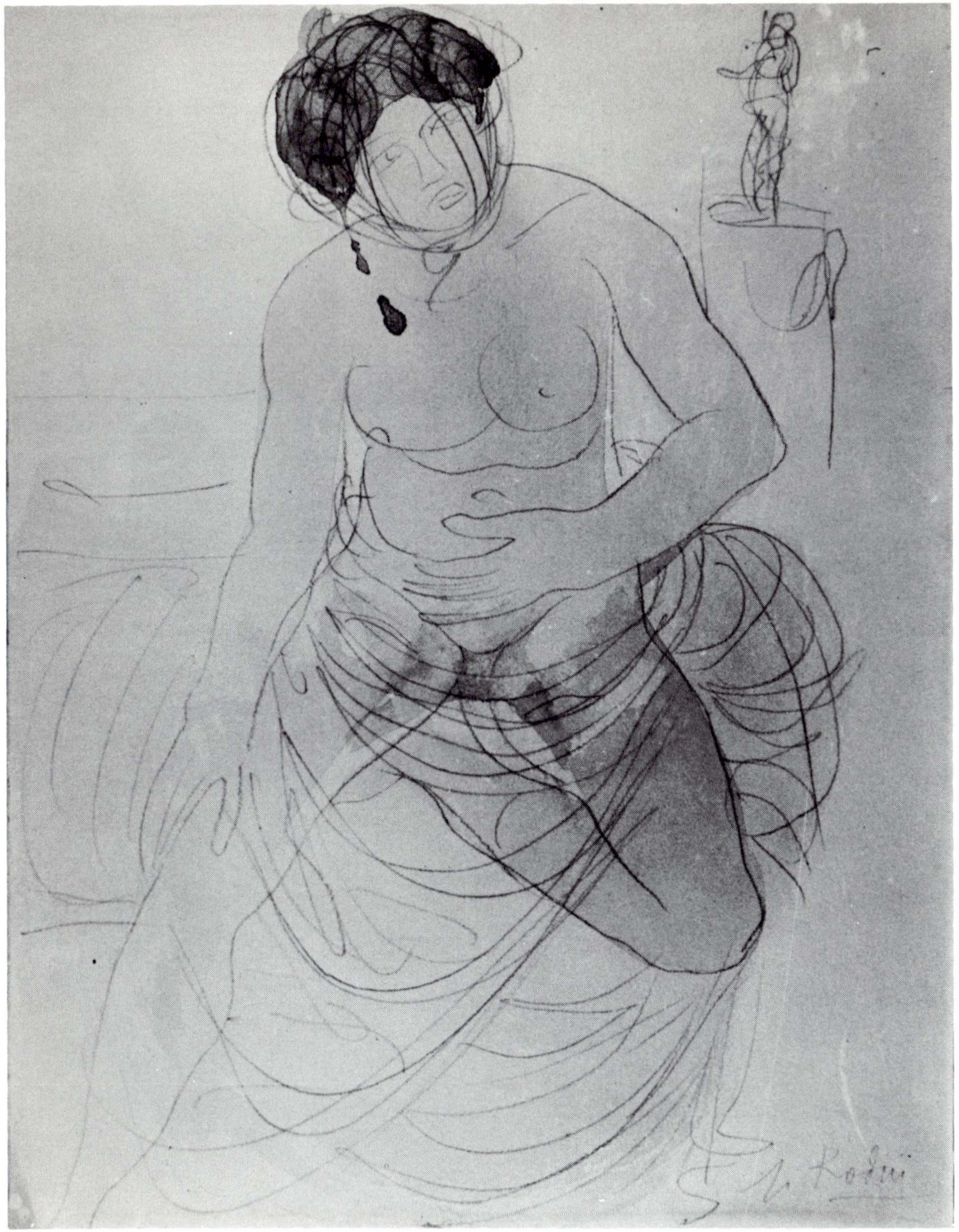

Nude Study

Pencil and watercolor

MUSEUM OF FINE ARTS, BUDAPEST, HUNGARY

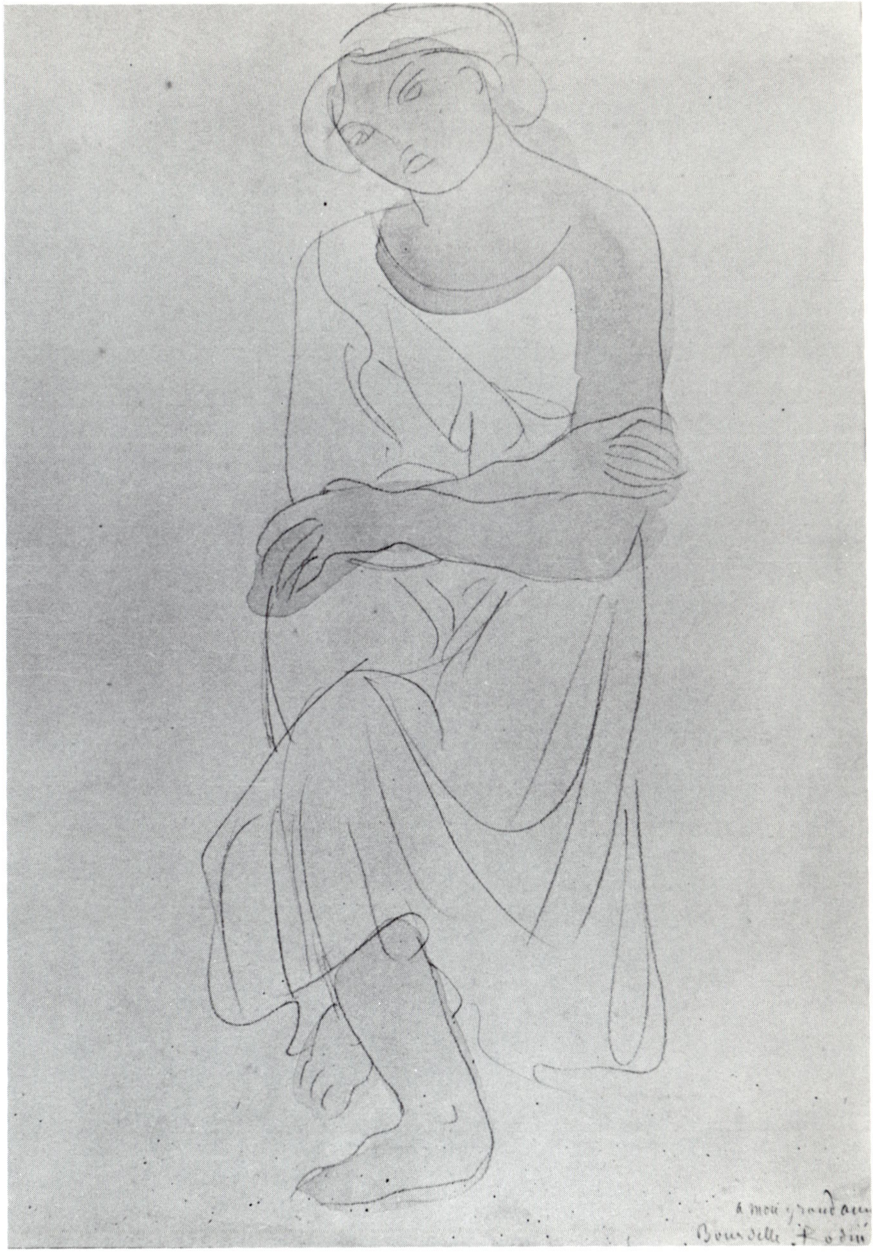

Seated Figure with Crossed Arms

Pencil and watercolor

THE BOURDELLE MUSEUM, PARIS, FRANCE

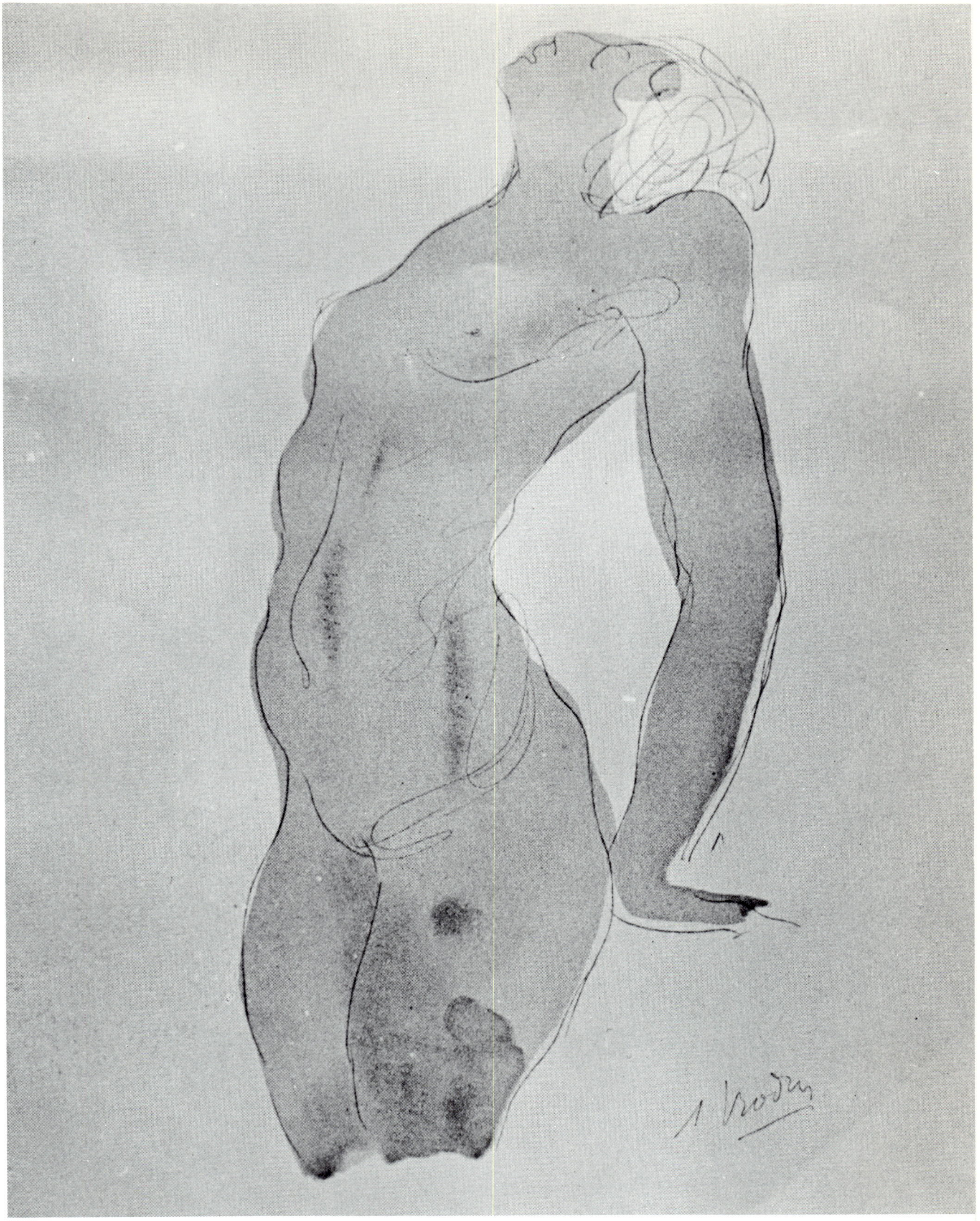

Figure Study

Pencil and watercolor

COURTESY RODIN MUSEUM, PHILADELPHIA, PA.

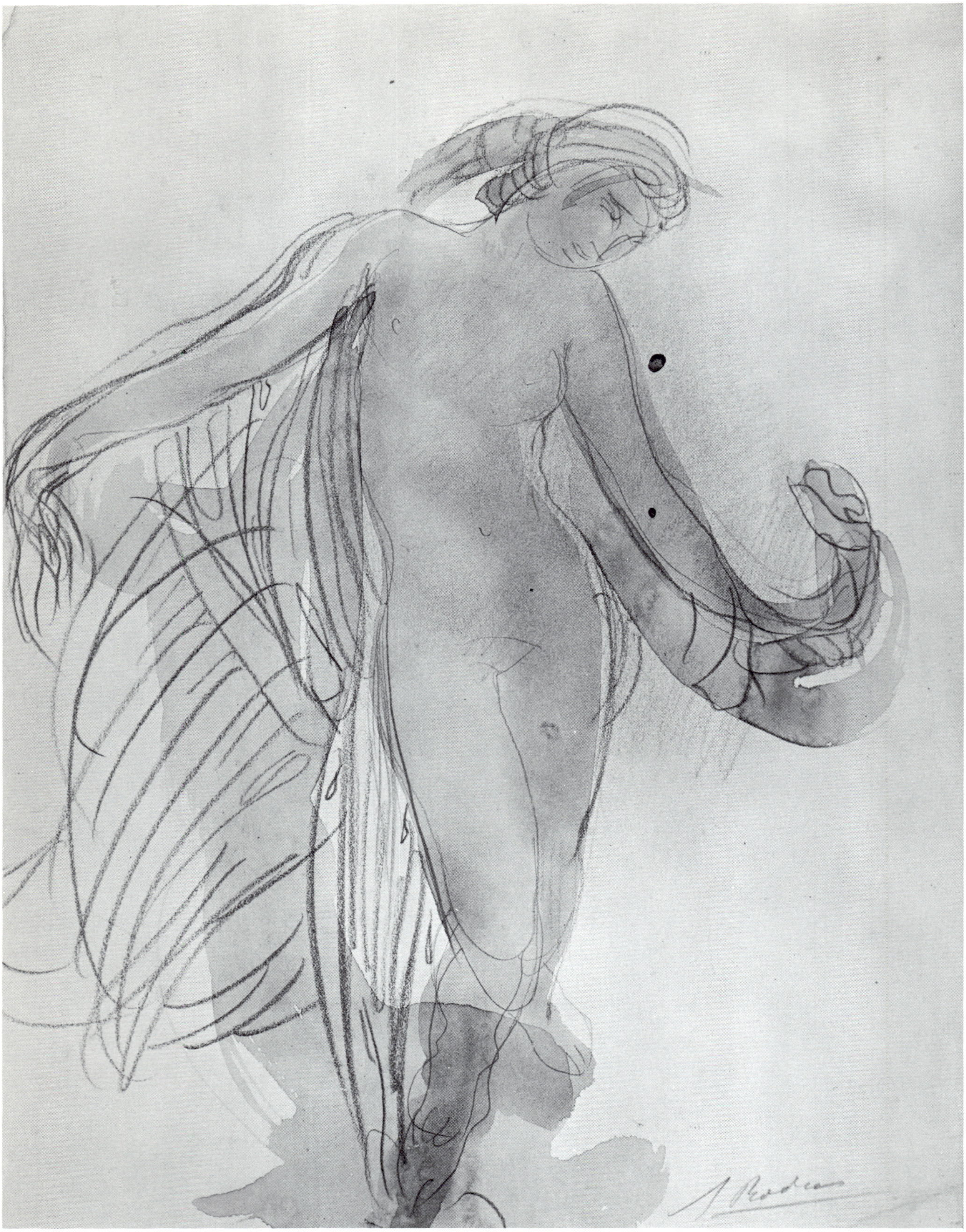

Figure Facing Forward

Pencil and watercolor

NATIONAL GALLERY OF ART, WASHINGTON, D.C.
GIFT OF MRS. JOHN W. SIMPSON

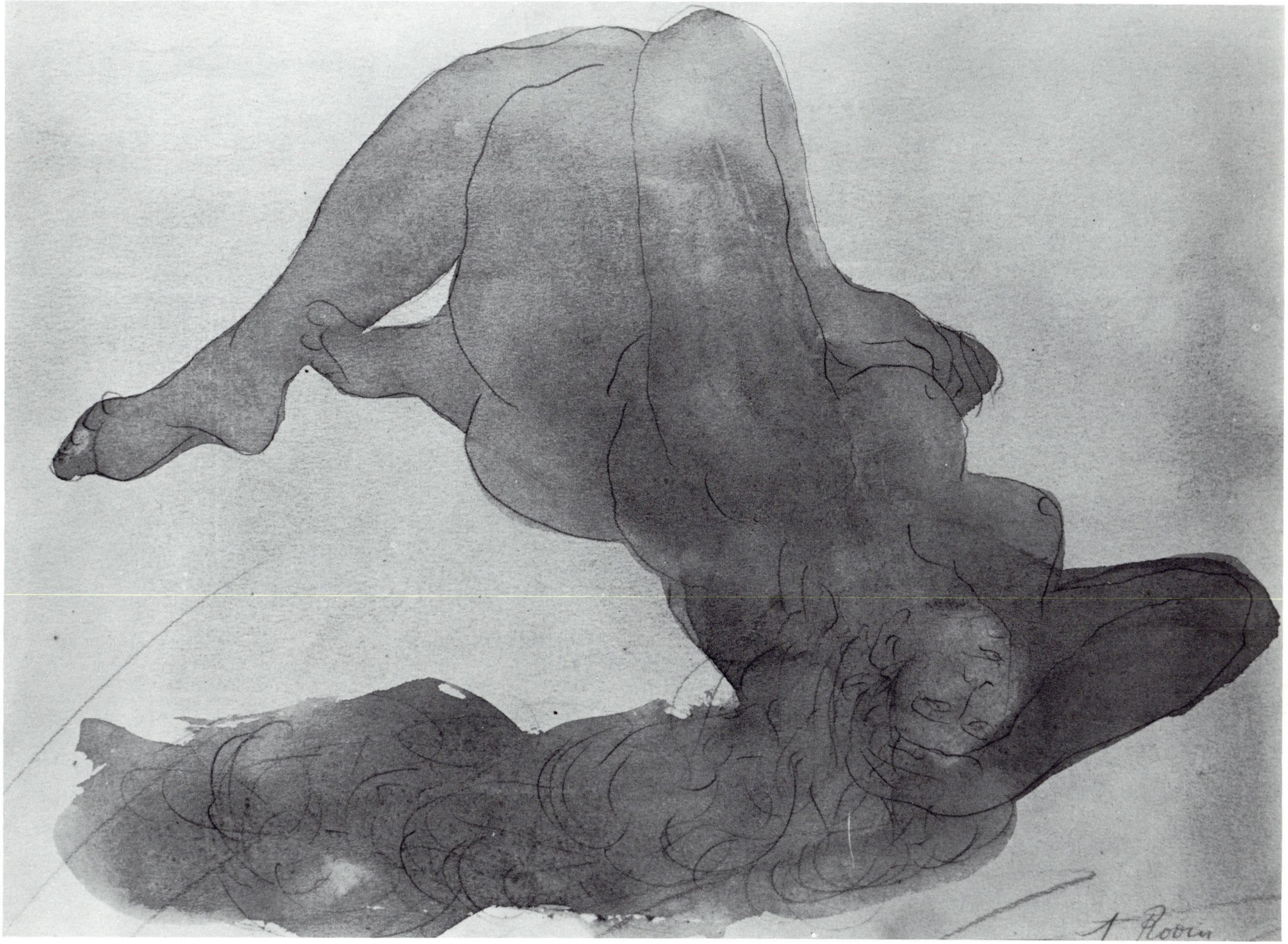

Nude

Pencil and colored wash

THE FINE ARTS GALLERY OF SAN DIEGO, SAN DIEGO, CALIF.

GIFT OF MRS. IRVING T. SNYDER

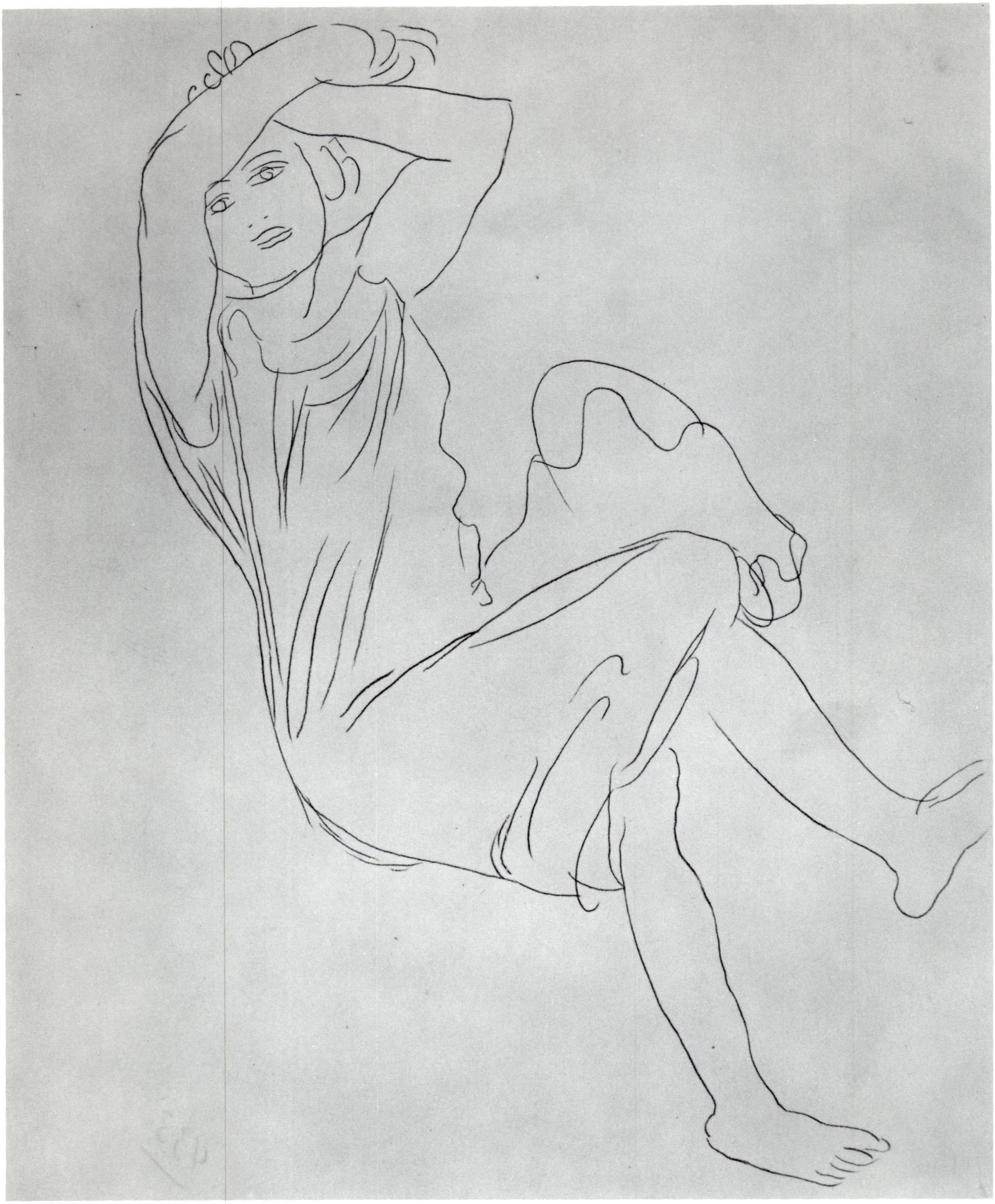

Seated Figure Study

Pen and ink

PHILADELPHIA MUSEUM OF ART, PHILADELPHIA, PA.

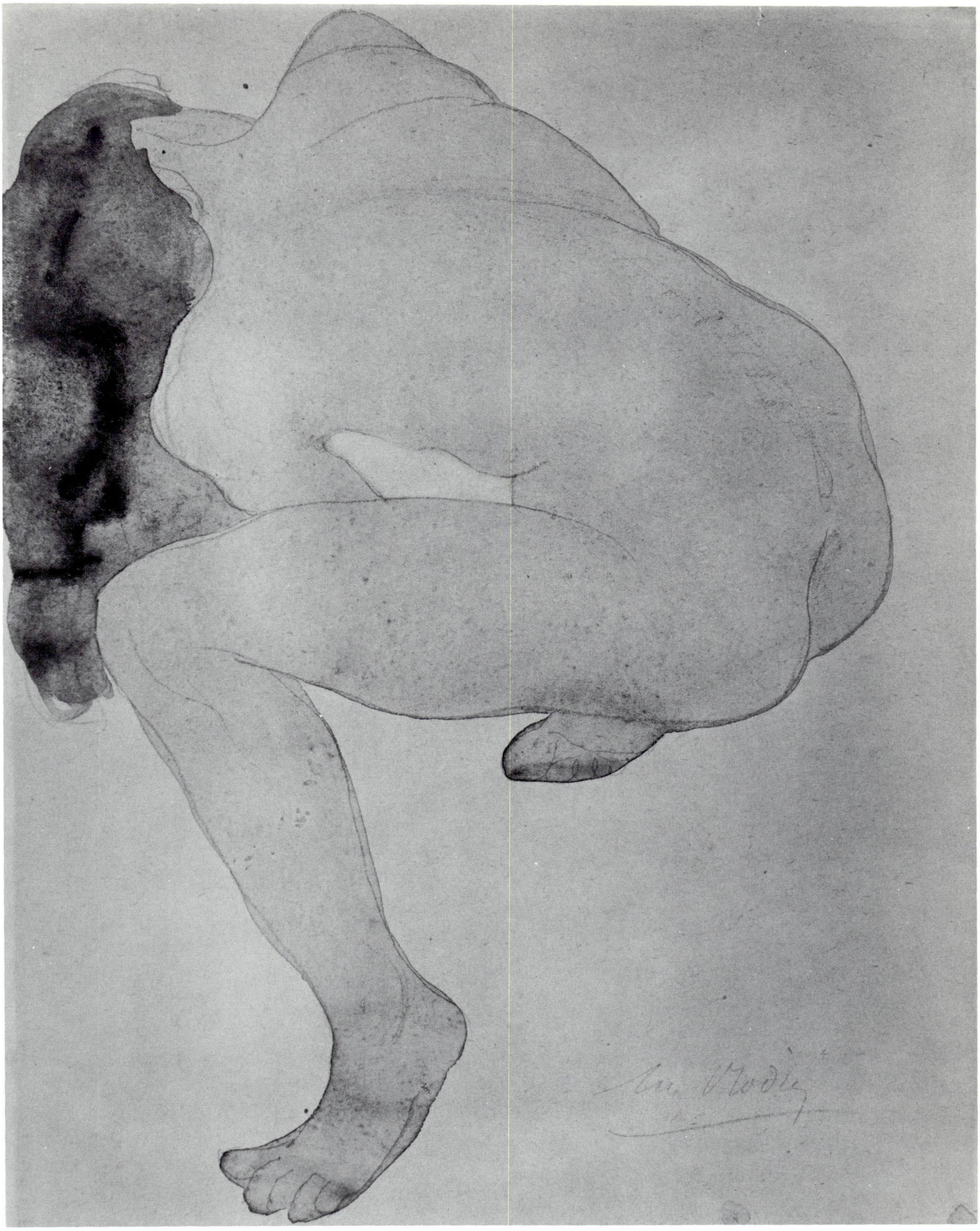

Nude with Flowing Hair

Pencil and water color

COURTESY RODIN MUSEUM, PHILADELPHIA, PA.

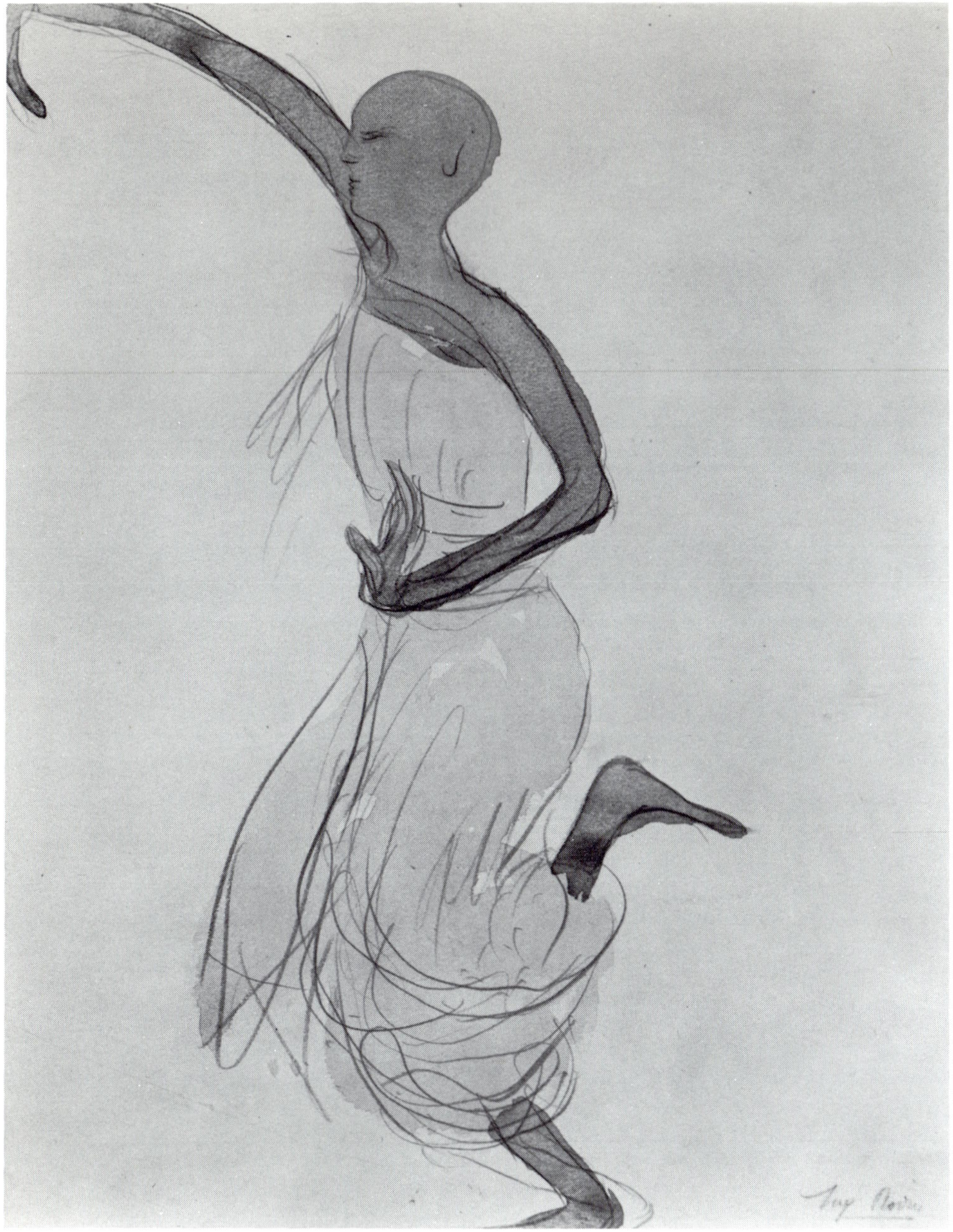

Dancer Facing Left

Pencil and watercolor

CHARLES E. SLATKIN GALLERIES, NEW YORK CITY, N.Y.

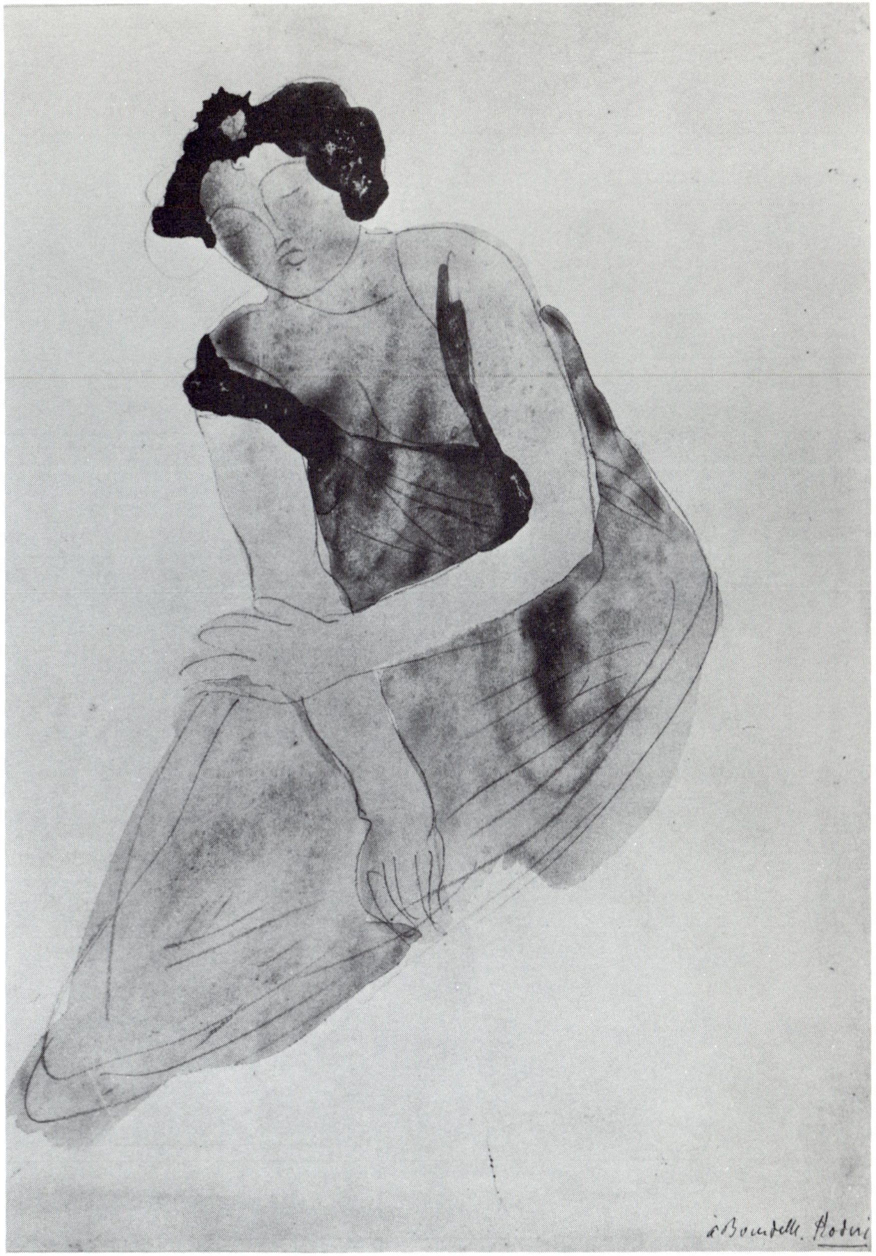

Seated Figure

Pencil and watercolor

BOURDELLE MUSEUM, PARIS, FRANCE

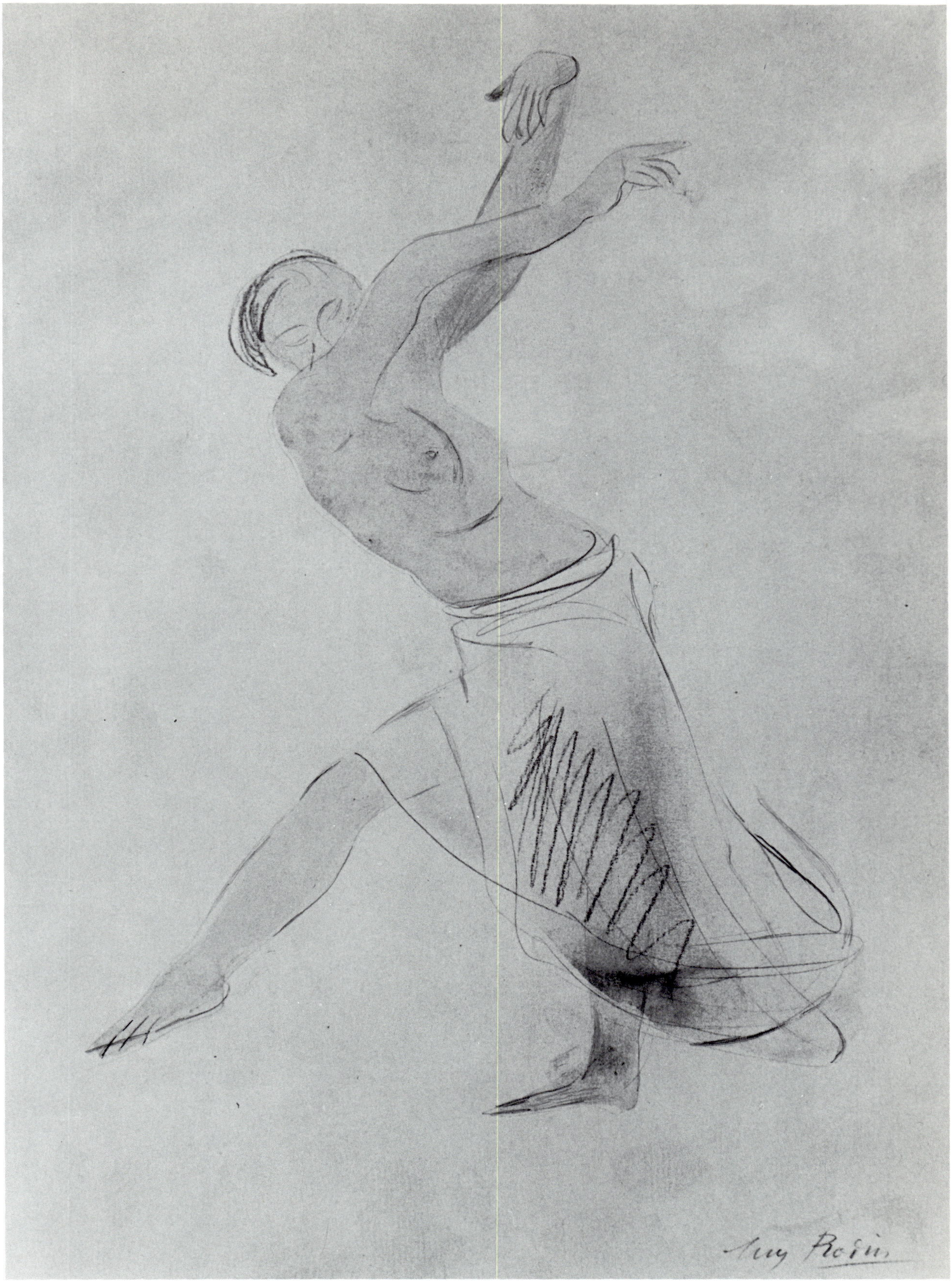

Cambodian Dancer

Pencil, crayon and pale wash

COURTESY MARY PICKFORD, BEVERLY HILLS, CALIFORNIA

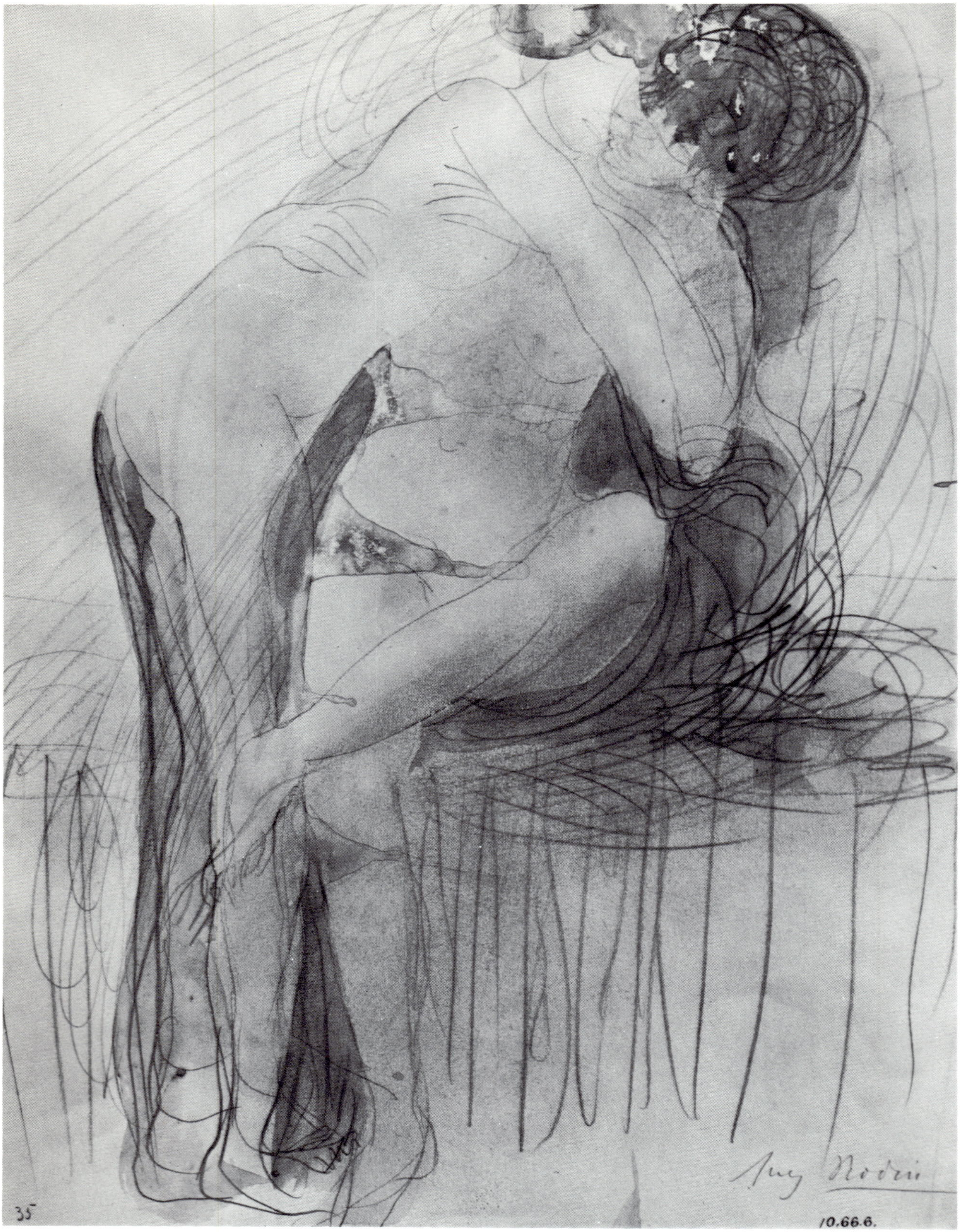

The Embrace

Lead pencil, watercolor and gouache

THE METROPOLITAN MUSEUM OF ART, NEW YORK CITY, N.Y.

KENNEDY FUND, 1910

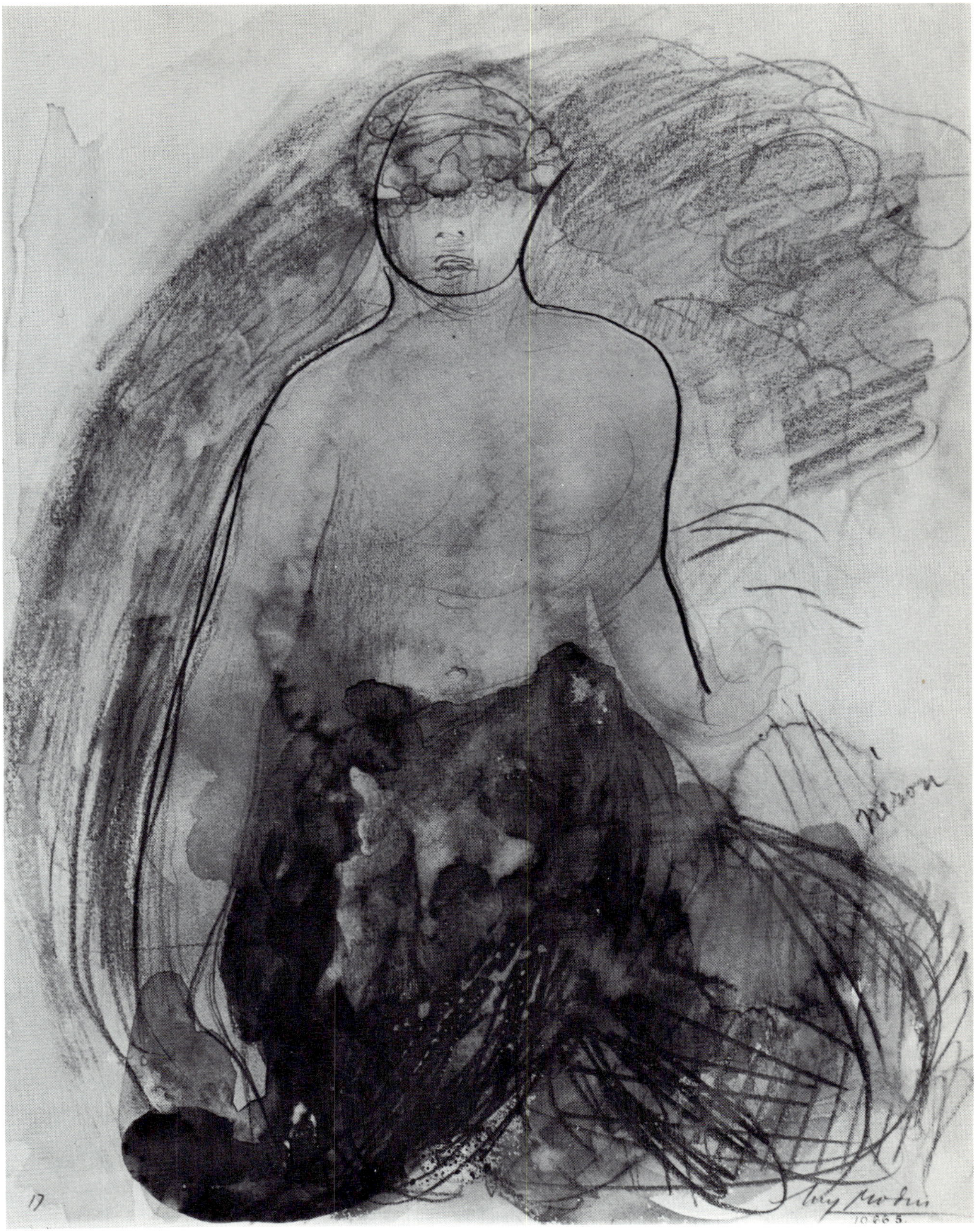

Nero

Pencil and gouache

THE METROPOLITAN MUSEUM OF ART, NEW YORK CITY, N.Y.

KENNEDY FUND, 1910

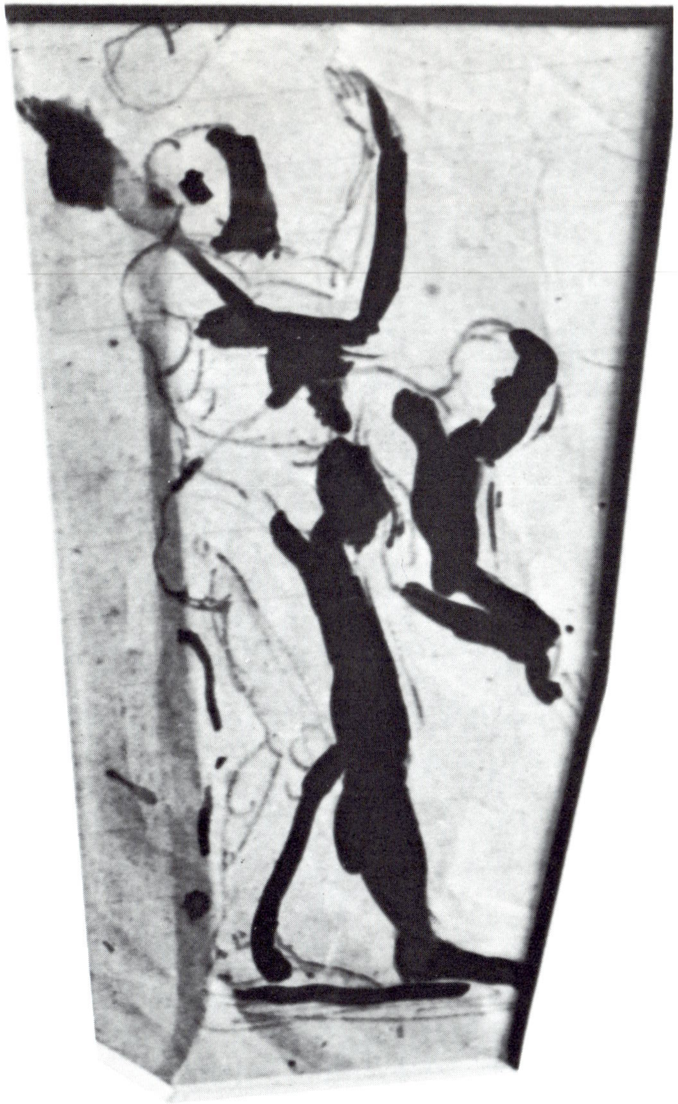

Two Figures

Pen and ink and wash

MUSEUM OF FINE ARTS, BUDAPEST, HUNGARY

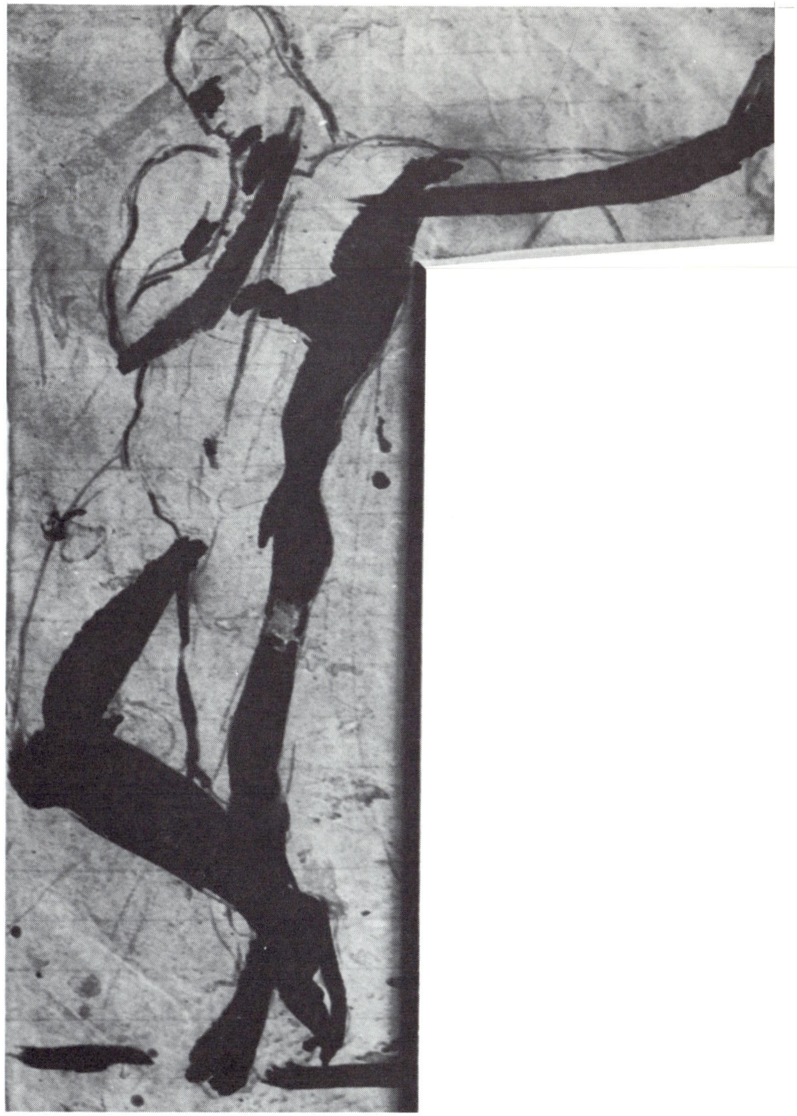

Standing Figure

Pencil and ink and wash

MUSEUM OF FINE ARTS, BUDAPEST, HUNGARY

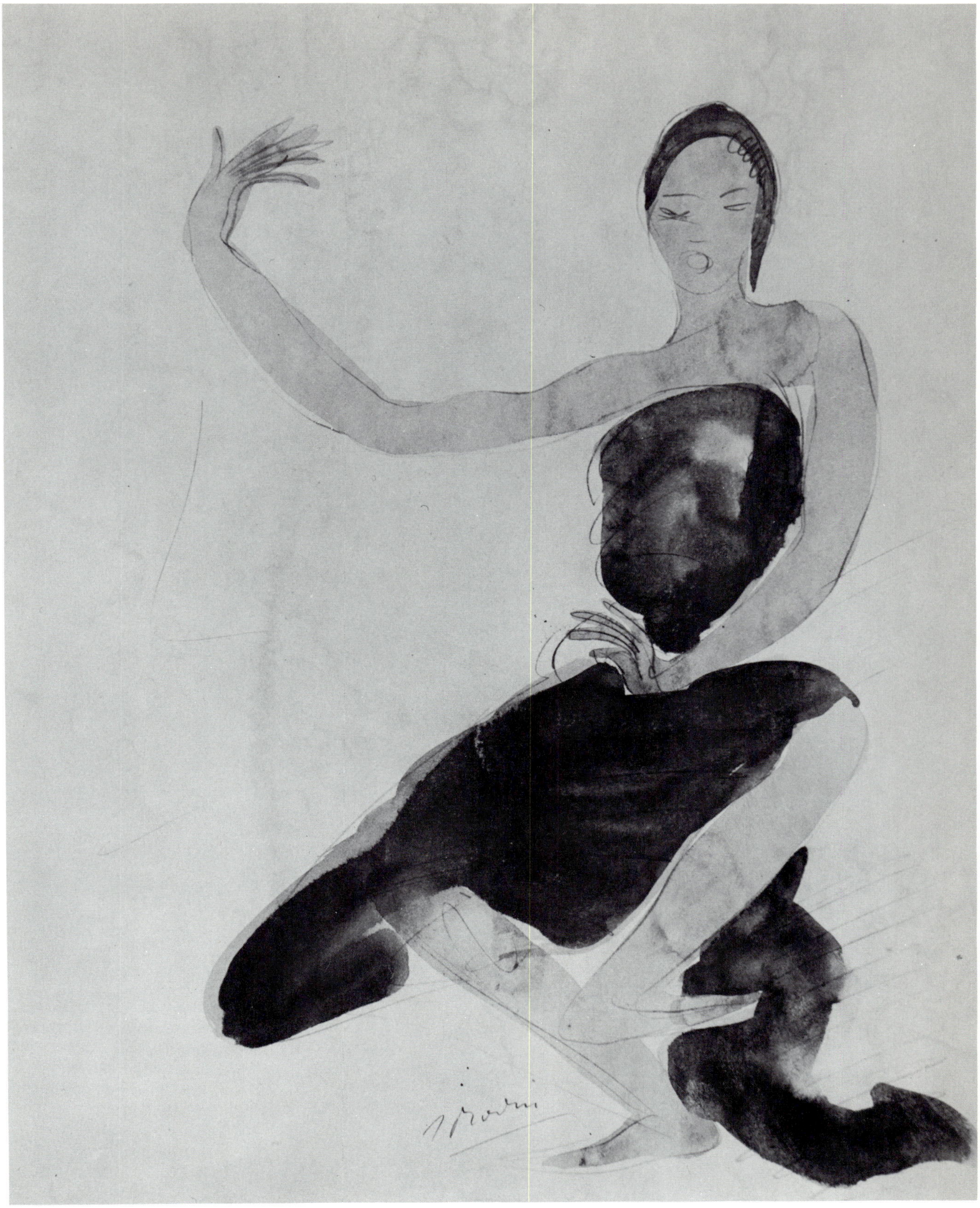

Dancer with Upraised Arm

Watercolor and pencil

THE BALTIMORE MUSEUM OF ART, BALTIMORE, MD.

CONE COLLECTION

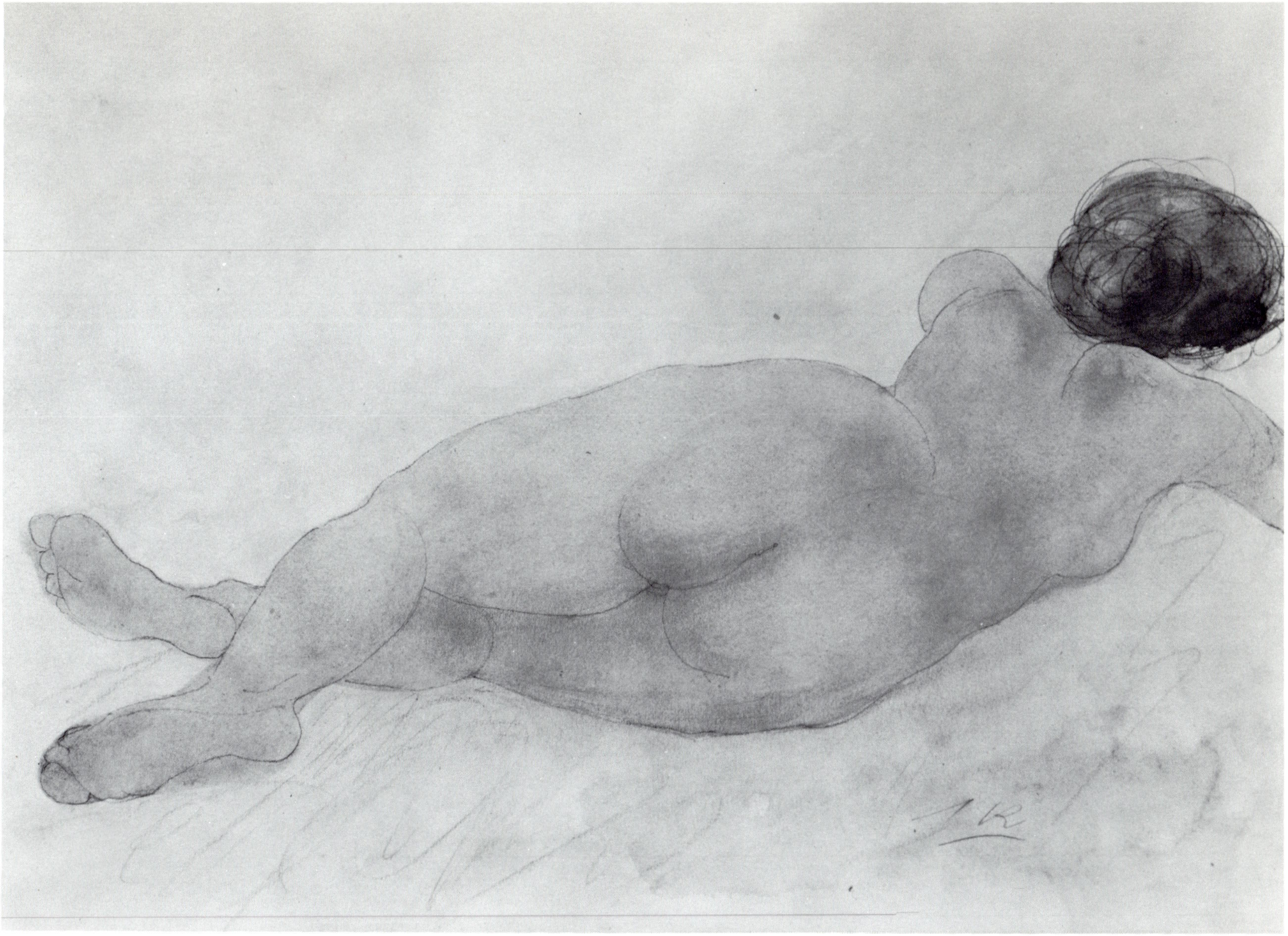

Reclining Nude

Pencil and watercolor

CHARLES E. SLATKIN GALLERIES, NEW YORK CITY, N.Y.

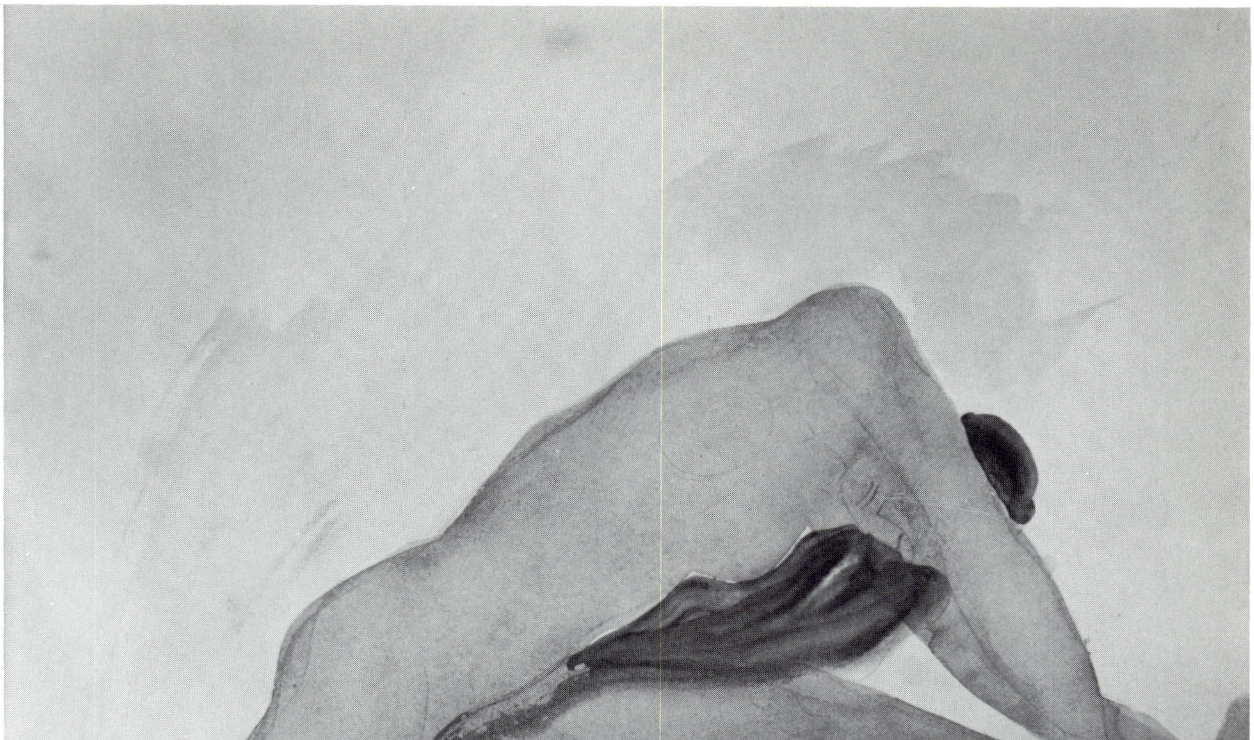

Figure Study

Sepia watercolor

T. E. HANLEY COLLECTION, BRADFORD, PA.

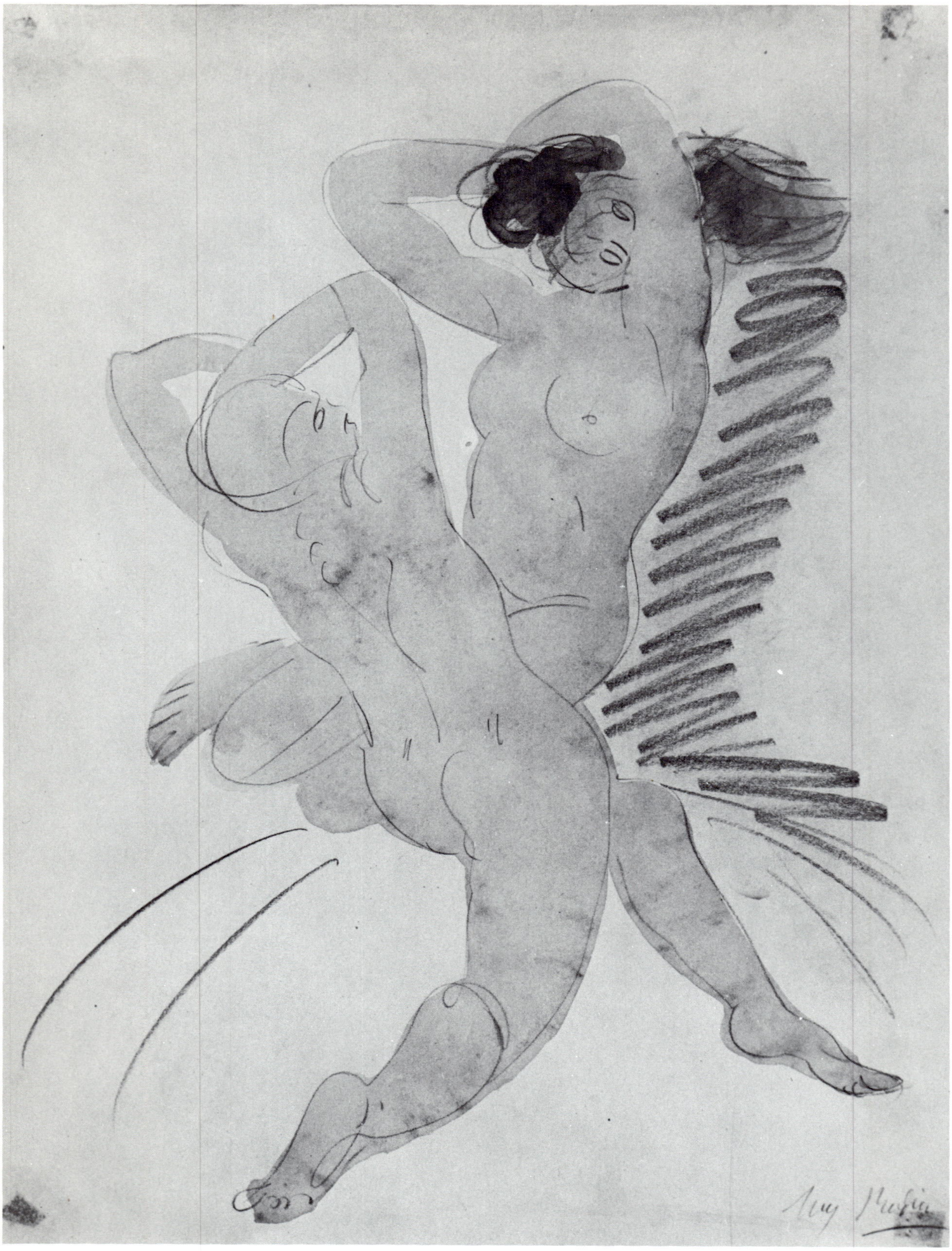

Two Figure Studies

Pencil, crayon and pink wash

COURTESY MARY PICKFORD, BEVERLY HILLS, CALIFORNIA

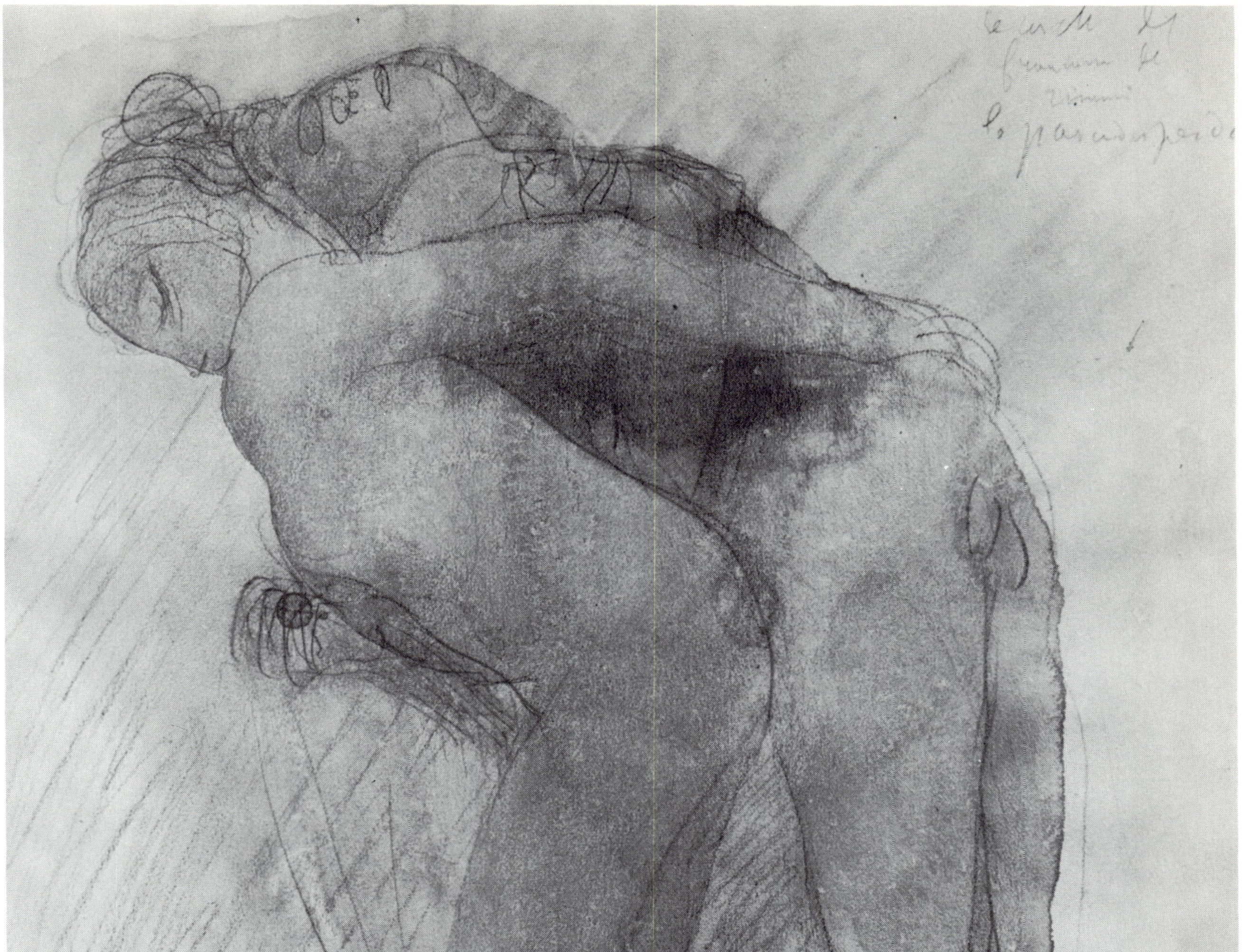

Paradise Lost

Pencil and wash

BOURDELLE MUSEUM, PARIS, FRANCE

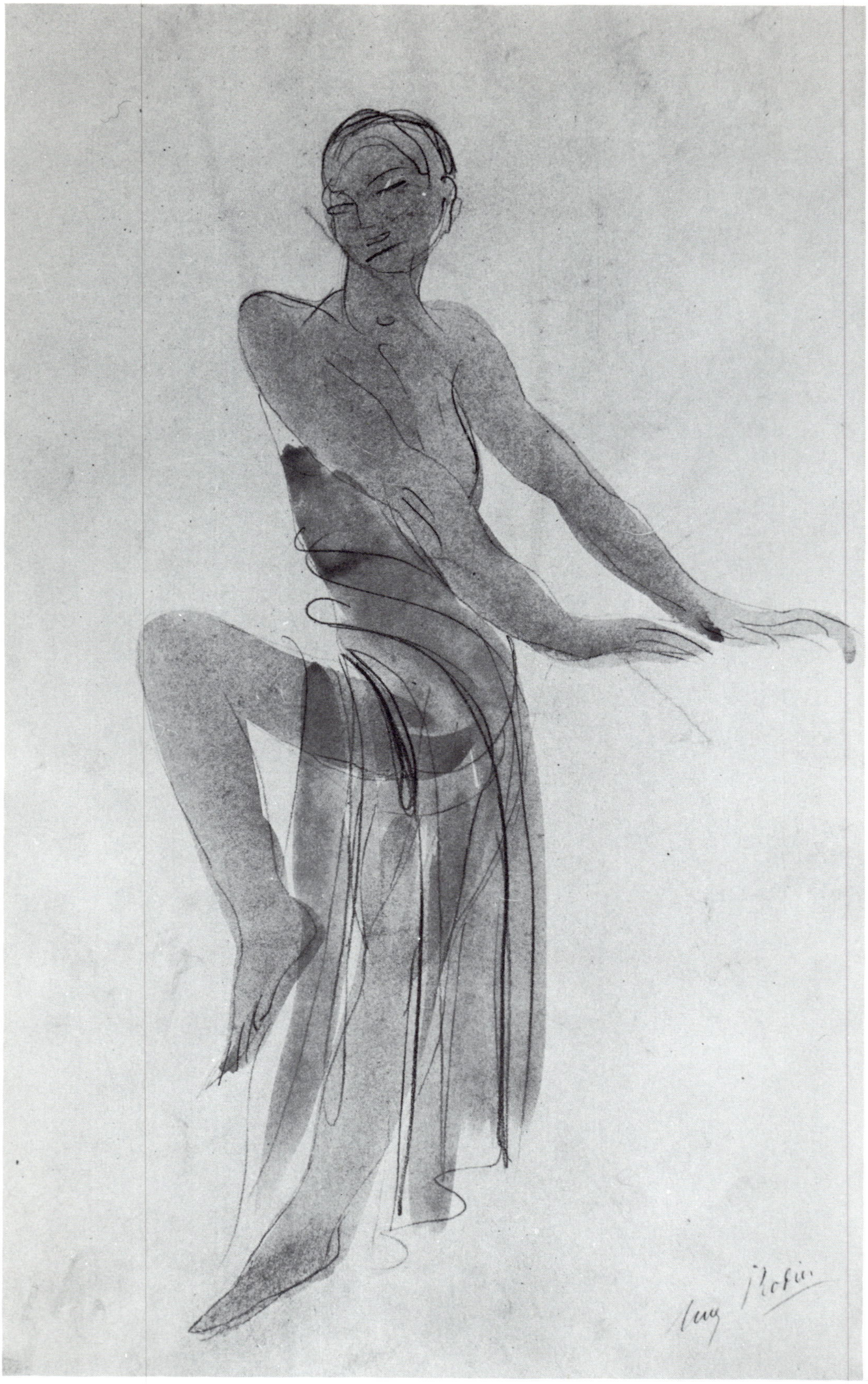

Dancer

Pencil and colored wash

THE BALTIMORE MUSEUM OF ART, BALTIMORE, MD.

CONE COLLECTION

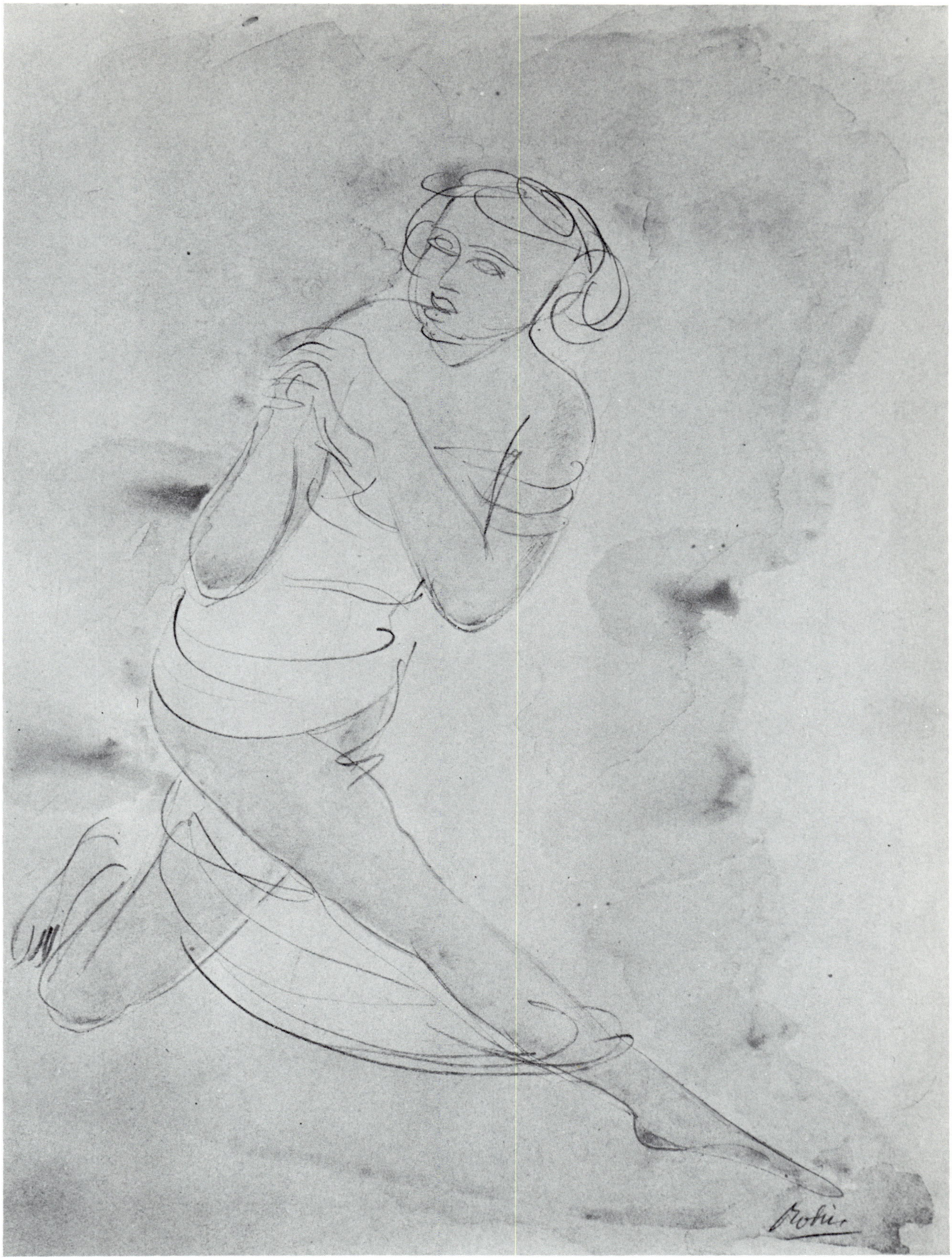

Figure Study

Pencil and watercolor

COURTESY MARY PICKFORD, BEVERLY HILLS, CALIFORNIA

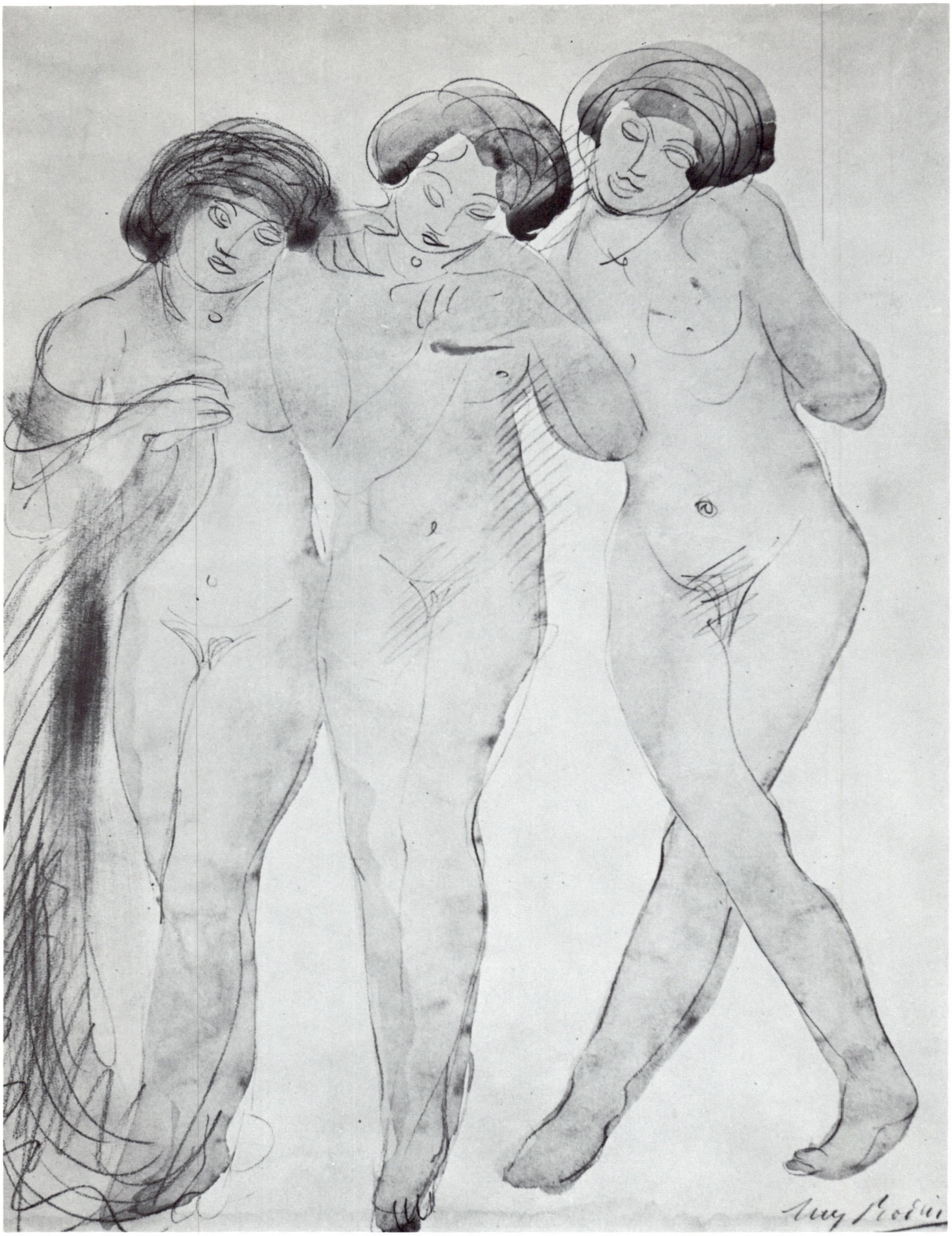

The Three Graces

Pencil, pink and gray watercolor

SANTA BARBARA MUSEUM OF ART, SANTA BARBARA, CALIFORNIA

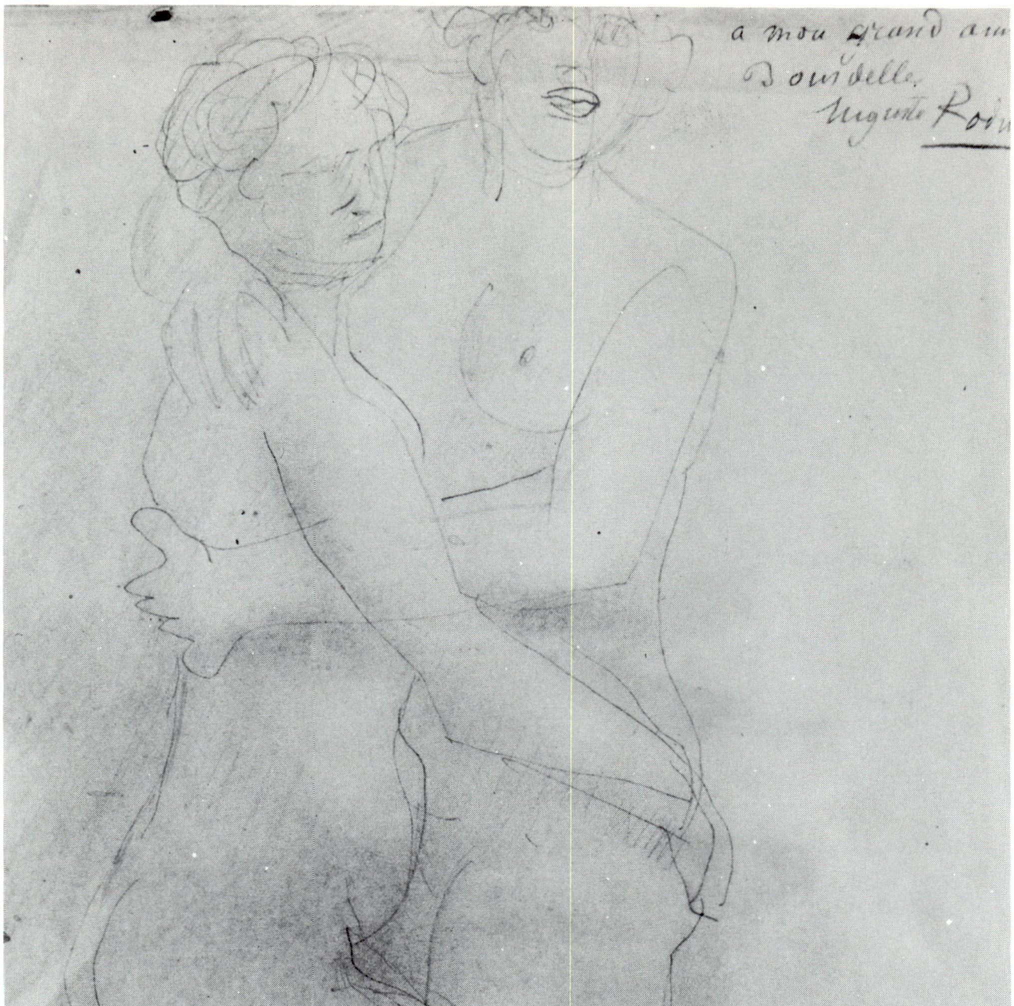

Two Young Women

Pencil

THE BOURDELLE MUSEUM, PARIS, FRANCE

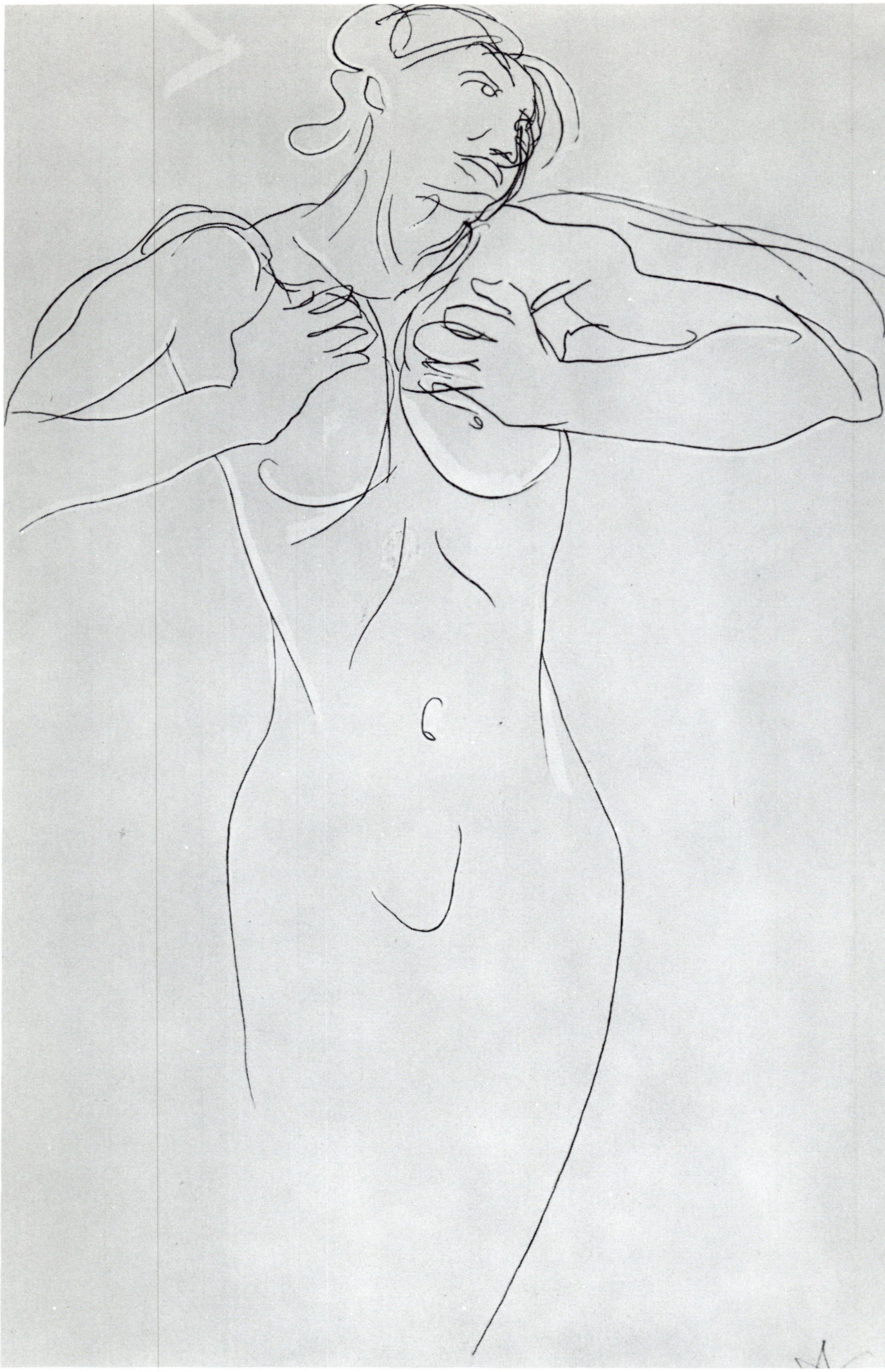

Woman Pressing Her Breasts

Pen and ink and gouache

PHILADELPHIA MUSEUM OF ART, PHILADELPHIA, PA.

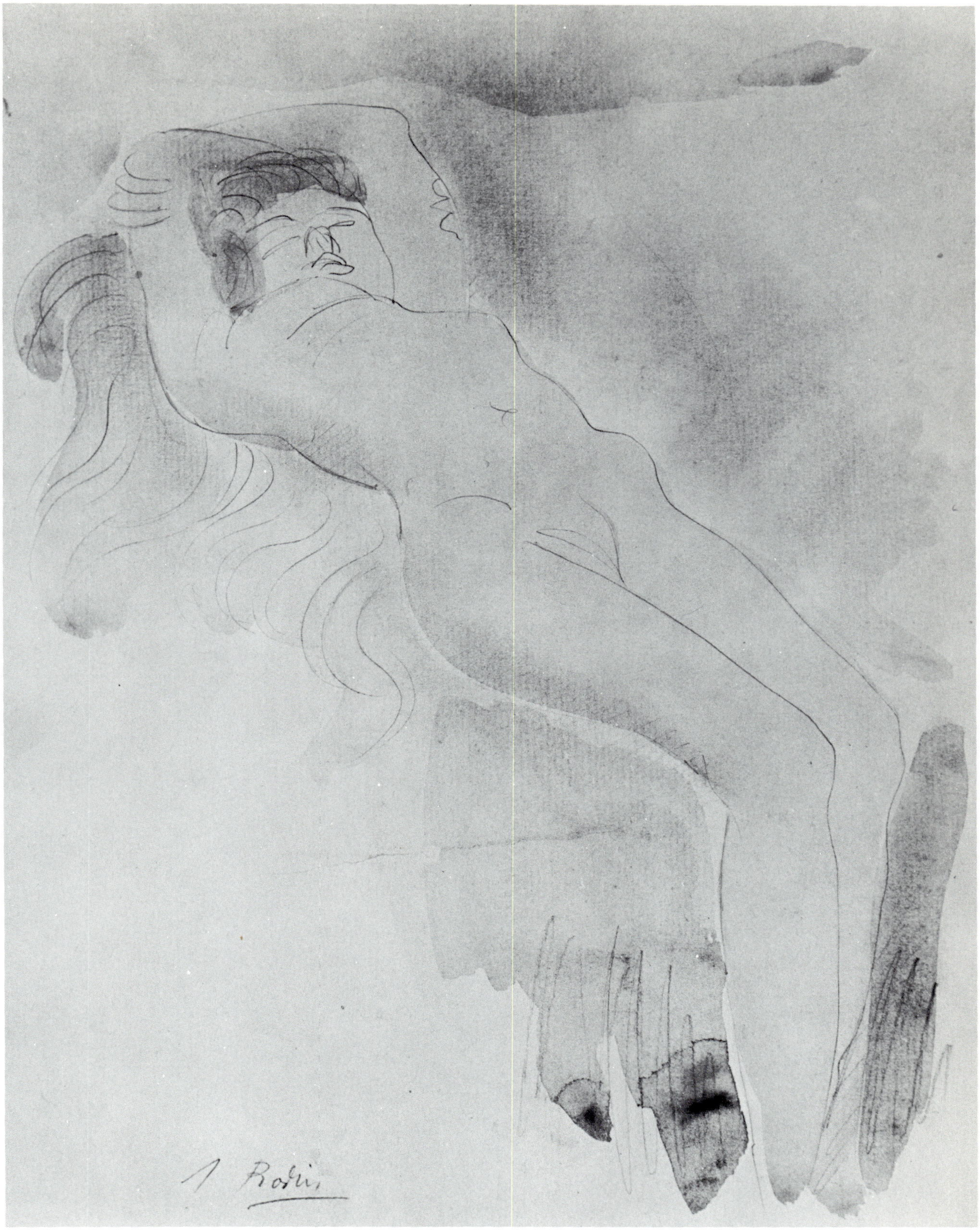

Resting Figure

Pencil, pink and gray wash

COURTESY MARY PICKFORD, BEVERLY HILLS, CALIFORNIA

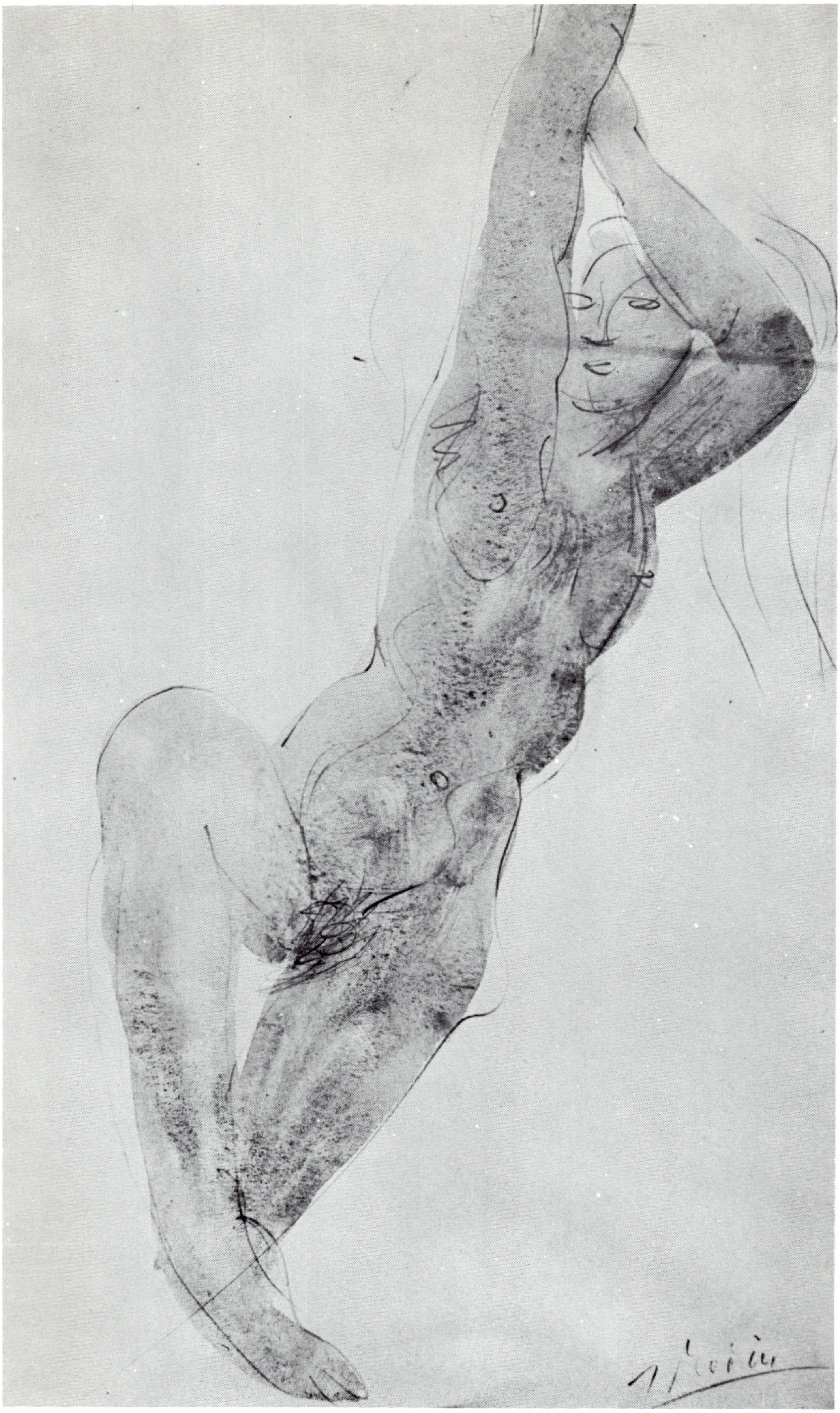

Nude

Pencil, pink and gray watercolor

SANTA BARBARA MUSEUM OF ART, SANTA BARBARA, CALIFORNIA

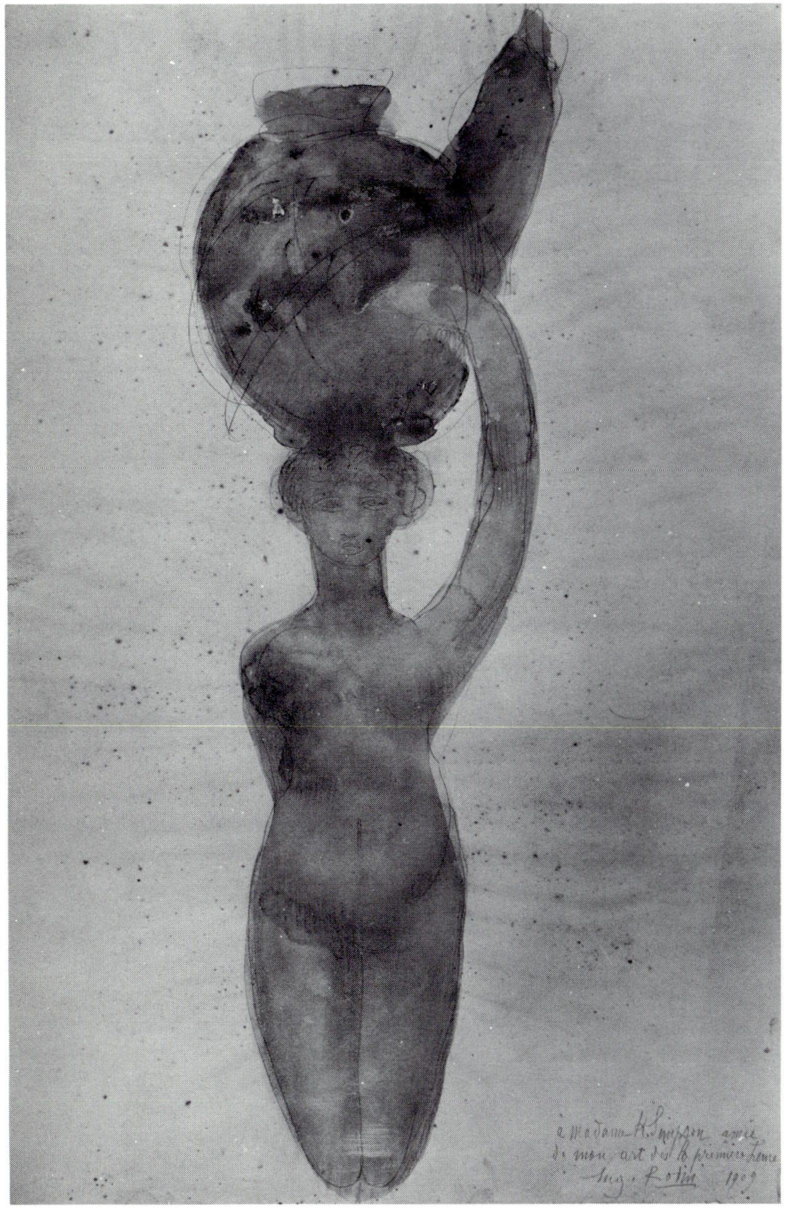

Nude Woman Carrying a Vase
Pencil and watercolor
NATIONAL GALLERY OF ART, WASHINGTON, D.C.
GIFT OF MRS. JOHN W. SIMPSON

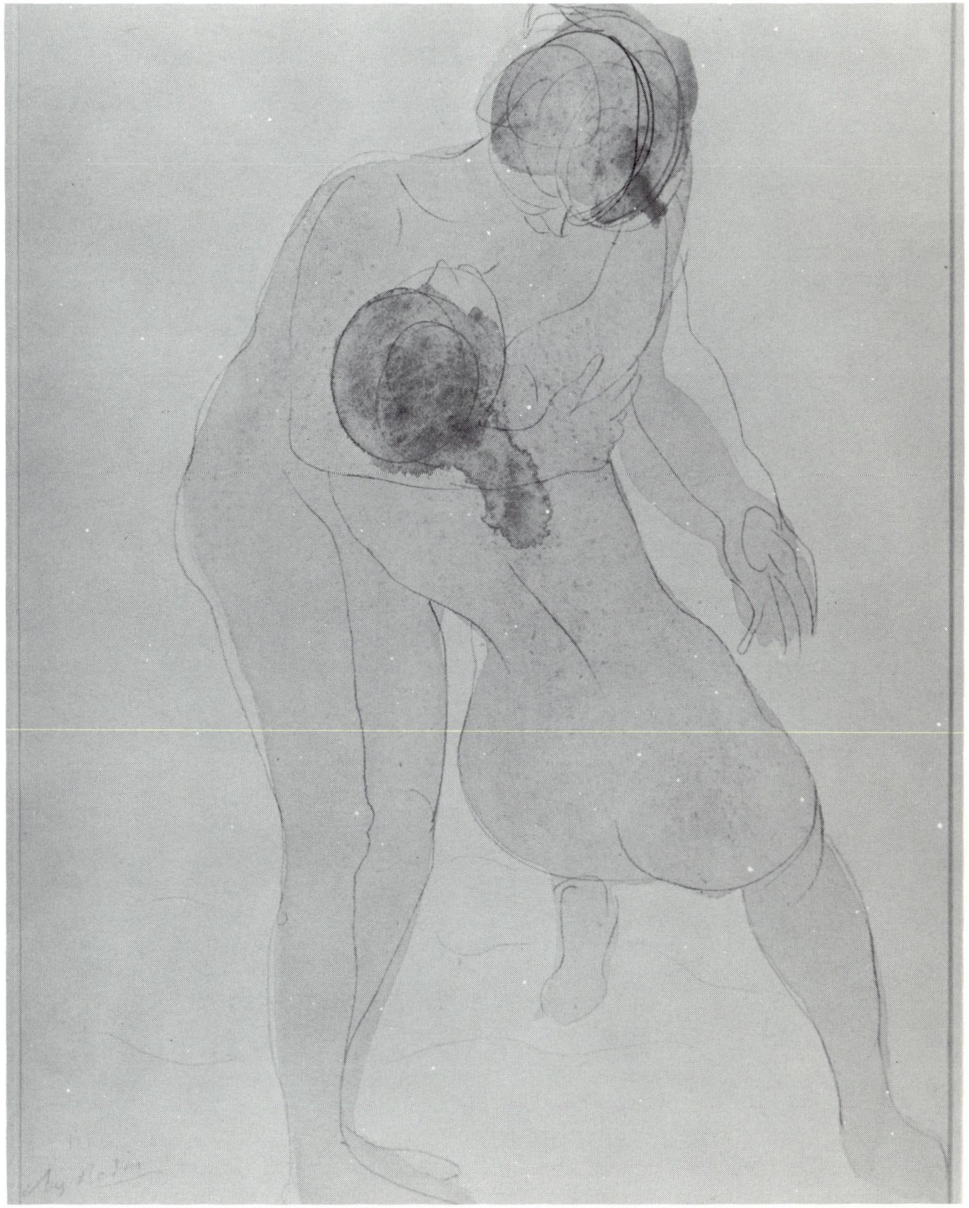

Two Figures
Pencil and colored wash
NATIONAL GALLERY OF ART, WASHINGTON, D.C.
GIFT OF MRS. JOHN W. SIMPSON

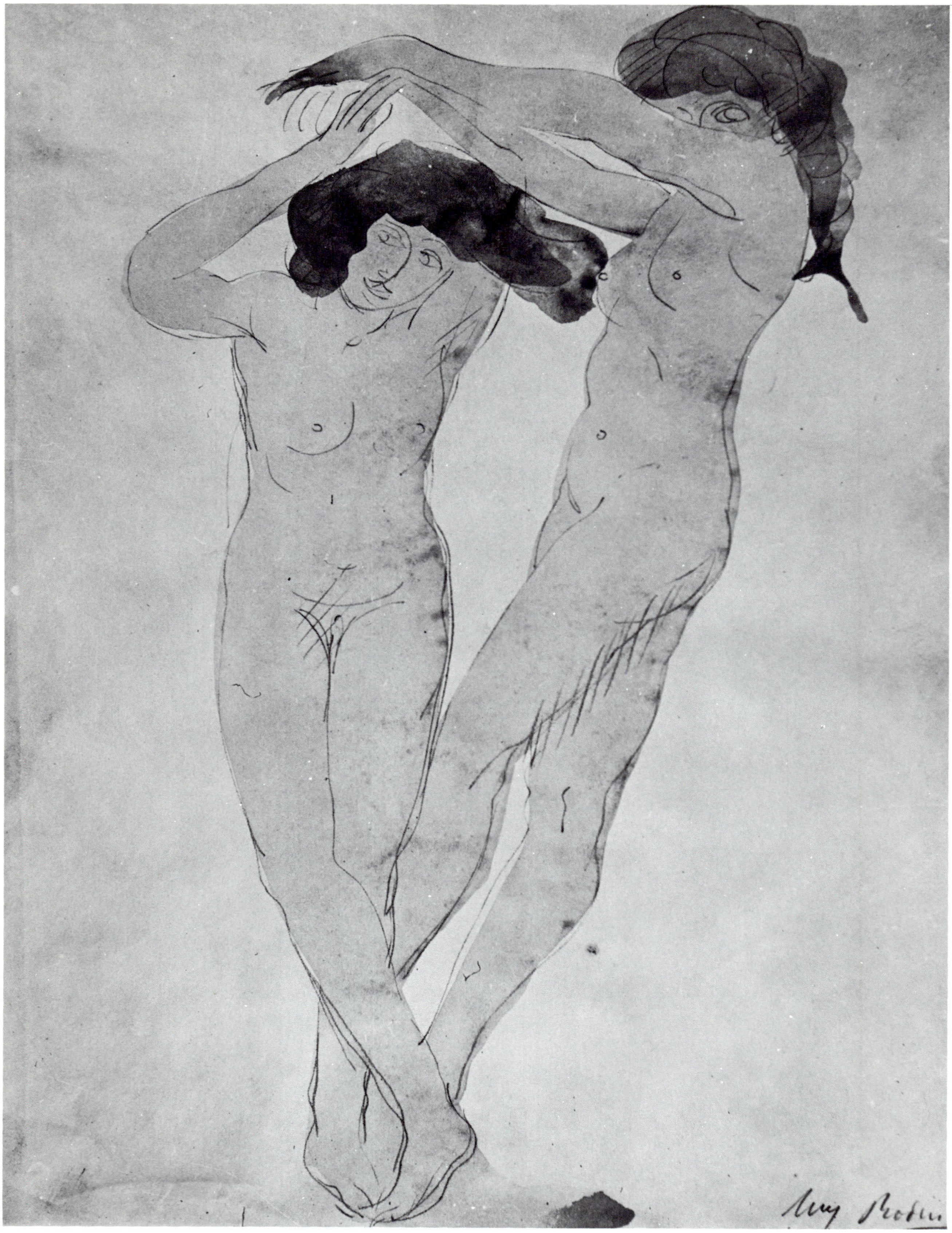

Two Female Nudes

Pencil, pink and gray watercolor

SANTA BARBARA MUSEUM OF ART, SANTA BARBARA, CALIFORNIA

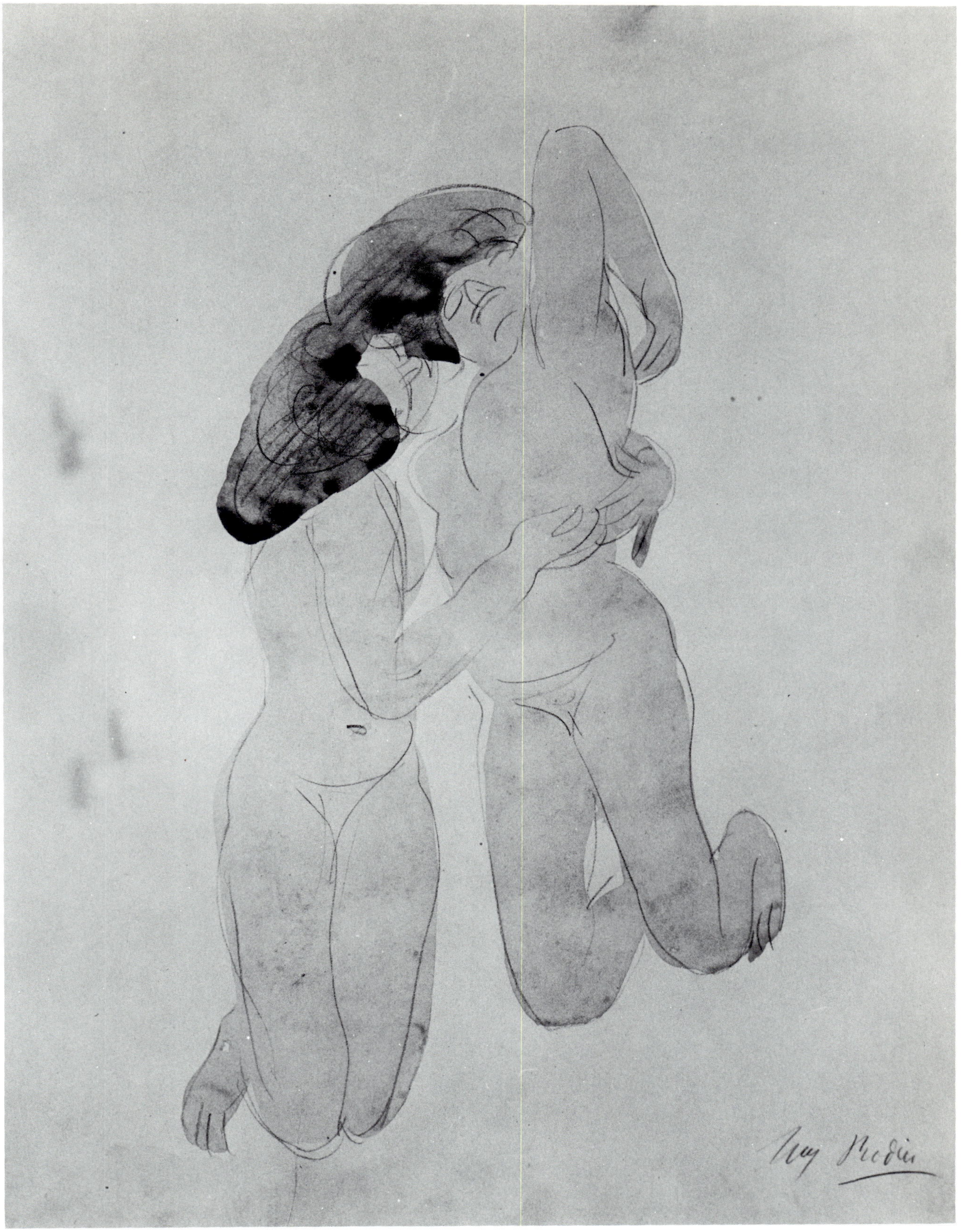

Two Figure Studies

Pencil, pen and ink, and pink wash

COURTESY MARY PICKFORD, BEVERLY HILLS, CALIFORNIA

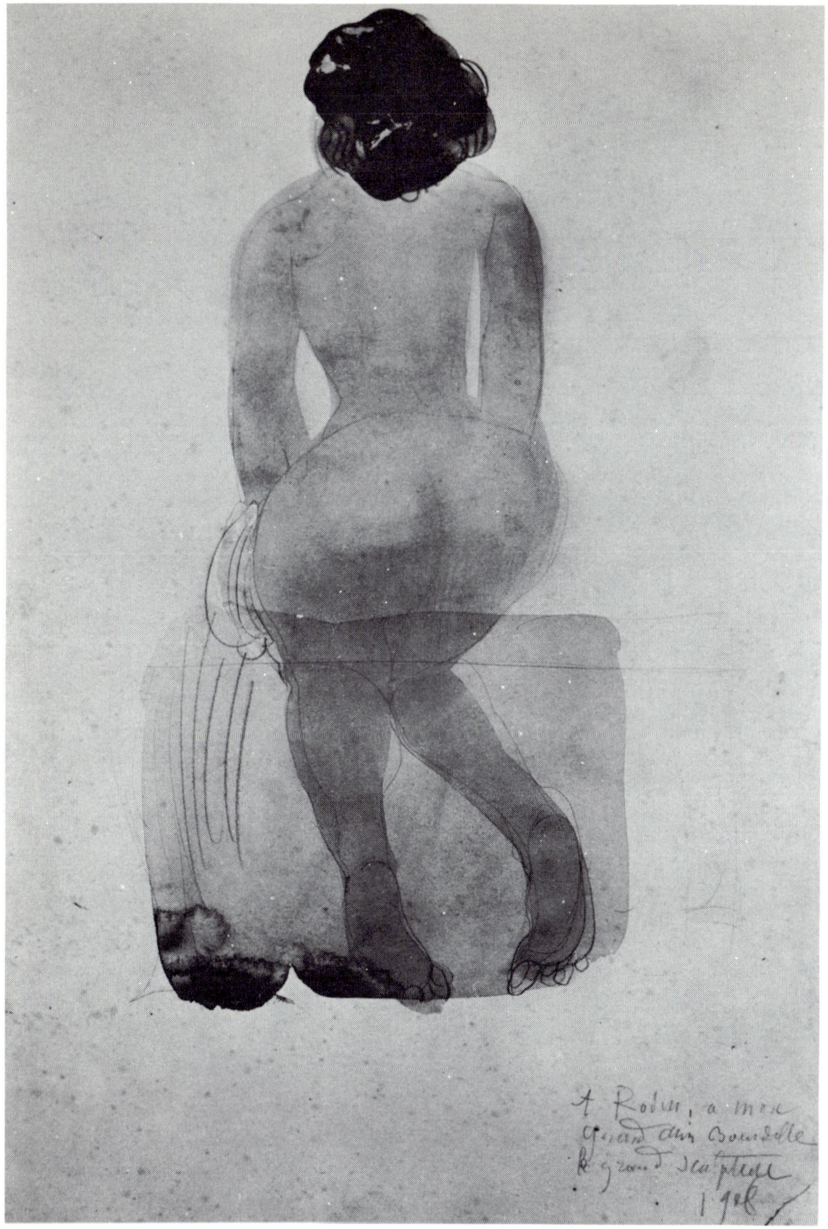

The Peach

Pencil and watercolor

BOURDELLE MUSEUM, PARIS, FRANCE

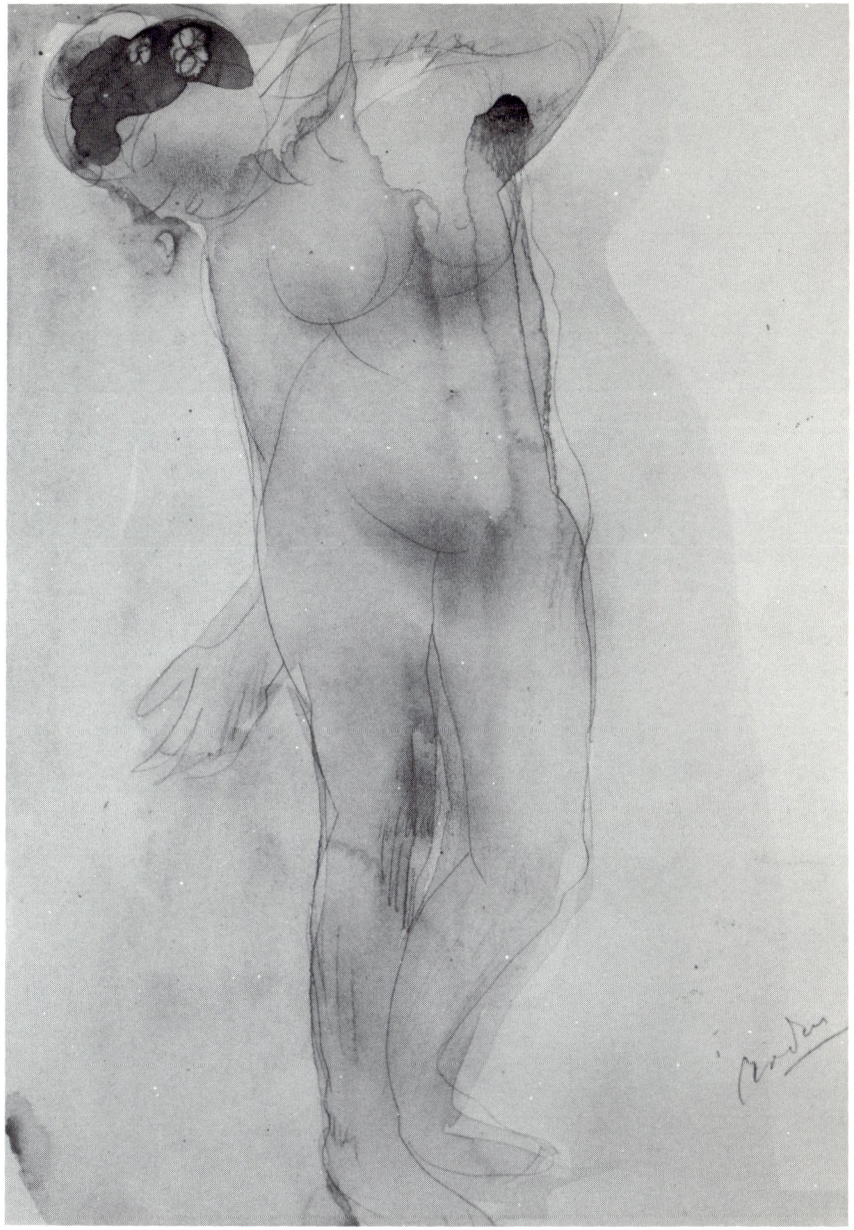

Standing Nude

Pencil and watercolor

COLLECTION MILLS COLLEGE ART GALLERY, OAKLAND, CALIFORNIA